T5-AFO-730

$ 8.98

Behold also the
ships, which
though they be
so great, and are
driven of fierce
winds, yet are
they turned about
with a very
Small Helm.

Small Helm Press
Petaluma, California

ATLANTIC OCEAN

NORWAY
SWEDEN
FINLAND
UNITED KINGDOM
DENMARK
SOVIET UNION (USSR)
IRELAND
NETHERLANDS
London
(EAST)
BELGIUM
GERMANY
POLAND
Berlin
Brussels
Cologne
Jena
Bonn •GERMANY
Paris
LUX.
Trier
CZECHOSLOVAKIA
FRANCE
AUSTRIA
HUNGARY
SWITZ.
ROMANIA
ITALY
YUGOSLAVIA
PORTUGAL
SPAIN
BULGARIA
ALBANIA
GREECE

EUROPE
CITIES WHERE MARX LIVED

chronology

1818   5 May: Karl Marx born in Trier
1835   to college at Bonn
1836   engaged to Jenny von West-
       phalen; in college at Berlin
1838   10 May death of father
1841   15 April receives his doctorate
1842   enters journalism in Cologne
       Oct.: denies he is promoting
       communism, promises to in-
       vestigate the subject
1843   marries; a few months later to
       Paris
1844   Friedrich Engels visits for ten
       days; Marx accepts commun-
       ism as label for his views
1845   expelled from France.

       To Brussels
1847   member of the Communist
       League
1848   February: *Communist Manifesto*
       March: expelled from Belgium.
       To Cologne
1849   expelled as a stateless subject.
       To London
1864   Working Men's International
       Association founded
1867   first volume of *Capital*
1881   December: death of wife, Jenny
1883   Jan.: death of daughter, Jenny
       March: death of Karl Marx
1895   death of Friedrich Engels

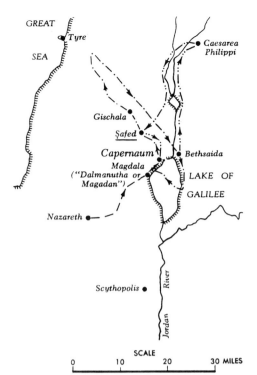

journeys in Israel

Journeys of Jesus traced in general way:

In his lifetime, Jesus lived in Israel except when, as a baby, his parents took him to Egypt to save his life.

During his ministry, he traveled in a small area.

Mark 1:16 Nazareth to Capernaum
7:17 Capernaum to Tyre territory 7:24
Back to Lake of Galilee and Decapolis
8:10 Across lake to Dalmanutha
8:22 Bethsaida to Caesarea Philippi 8:27
9:2 To Mount of transfiguration
9:30 Galilean travel
9:33 To Capernaum

SOME JOURNEYS OF JESUS
(According to Mark)

Galilee is the northern part of Israel.
Judea is the southern part of Israel.

Gospel of John:
To Nazareth, to Jordan baptism,
 Nazareth, Cana
Nazareth to Capernaum to Jerusalem
Perean detour
Into Judean country
To Sychar (Shechem), Nazareth, Cana
Final departure from Galilee
To Jerusalem via the Jordan Valley.
To other side of Jordan
To Bethany to raise Lazarus from dead
To concealment at Ephraim
To Jerusalem where he was crucified

SOME JOURNEYS OF JESUS
(According to John)

The two map diagrams of the journeys of Jesus are used with permission from RAND McNALLY'S HISTORICAL ATLAS OF THE HOLY LAND ©1959.

by the same author

CHINA: The Lion and the Dragon
a personal interpretation

and forthcoming book

CHAMELEON TACTICS
how liberation theology works

MARX OR JESUS

TWO MEN—TWO PLANS

by Pearl Evans

Small Helm Press
Petaluma, California 94952

dedicated to

Nealy, Jesse
Kurt, Rachel
Kelly, Kerry, Kristin
Justin, Andrew, Melissa
and their future

Library of Congress Cataloging in Publication Data

Evans, Pearl, 1927-
    Marx or Jesus: two men—two plans / by Pearl Evans
    p.   cm.
    Bibliography: p.
    Includes index.
    ISBN 0-938453-03-3: $17.95
    1. Communism and Christianity. 2. Marx, Karl, 1818-1883.
3. Jesus Christ. 4. Communism. 5. Christianity. I. Title.
HX536.E95 1989
335.4' 1--dc19   89-5866 CIP

Following *The Chicago Manual of Style,* Small Helm Press
does not capitalize pronouns for deity.

Matthew 13 scripture quotation taken from the Holy Bible,
New International Version (NIV), Copyright ©1973, 1978
by New York International Bible Society. Used by permission.
Except where noted otherwise (such as King James Version [KJV]),
other scripture quotations are from the New King James Version (NKJ),
Copyright ©1979, 1980, 1982 by Thomas Nelson, Inc., Publisher.

All rights reserved, including the right of reproduction in whole
or in part in any form except for brief passages in book reviews

Copyright © 1989 by Pearl Evans
Design by Small Helm Press

This book may be ordered by mail from the publisher.
Please include two dollars for shipping.
Small Helm Press
622 Baker Street
Petaluma, California 94952

Manufactured in the United States of America
ISBN 0-938453-03-3
Library of Congress Catalog Card Number: 89-5866 CIP
10 9 8 7 6 5 4 3 2 1

contents

author's point of view

Here you meet two dynamos, Marx and Jesus.

Though their desired goals appear similar, my position is that their motivation, their foundations, and the practical outcome of their teachings oppose each other.

You will learn about the lives of Marx and Jesus, and about their principles, their targeted enemies, their influence, their polarity. And you will read the full texts of their manifestos: the communist manifesto of Marx (and Engels) and what I consider to be the manifesto of Jesus. In the manifestos you will read in their own words the two men's basic philosophies and ultimate objectives for the world.

After long months of seeking the significant in Karl Marx's life and teachings, I do not claim to be a casual onlooker. For, although the man of history has become a "real" person to me, I maintain that the evidence about his character and his stated intentions reveal a rebellious heart. I subscribe to Jesus' message that from the individual heart flows all that is good or evil in this world. In this volume I offer you my convictions as a solid springboard upon which to bounce off your ideas and from which to dive in either direction for deeper exploration.

When you learn what these worldchangers stand for, you will recognize the source of many ideas you encounter.

May you find this topic as fascinating as I have.

Pearl Evans

PART A

AN OVERVIEW
MARX OR JESUS

chapter 1. their principles

CHART 1: BOURGEOIS, PROLETARIAN

FOR REFERENCE: The reader needs to understand these terms: *bourgeois* and *proletarian; bourgeoisie* and *proletariat.*

Bourgeois and *proletarian* are nouns that refer to people. *The bourgeois* is a middle class person or middle class people with social behavior and political views influenced by private property interest; bourgeois can be singular or plural. *The proletarian* is a laborer with nothing to sell but his labor. (Plural is *proletarians.*)

Bourgeois and *proletarian* can also be adjectives to describe something as having middle class attributes, such as *bourgeois values.*

While the bourgeois and proletarians are people, the *bourgeoisie* and the *proletariat* are economic classes: the middle class and the working class, respectively.

their principles*

MARX OR JESUS

singleminded pursuit

Marx and Jesus buck the society of their day. Both know who they are, where they're headed, and how they will get there. They are strategists. They let nothing stand in the way of the pursuit of their goals and cannot be distracted from them. They sacrifice. And they ask the same of their followers—uncompromising, wholehearted loyalty. Even today.

Marx reveals this side of his character in the following questionnaire filled out for his daughter, Laura:**

Your favorite virtue: *Simplicity*
Your favorite virtue in man: *Strength*
Your favorite virtue in woman: *Weakness*
Your idea of happiness: *To fight*
Your idea of misery: *Submission*
The vice you excuse most: *Gullibility*
The vice you detest most: *Servility*
Your favorite color: *Red*

As Marx goes down the line, he fills out the blanks. When he comes to the one that says "your chief characteristic," he probably doesn't ponder long. As with anyone who possesses this number-one trait, he can immediately write this answer: "Singleness of purpose." And without needing great insight, when you read about his life, you will say the same about this man.

Jesus, also singleminded, says, "The lamp of the body is the eye. If therefore your eye is [single], your whole body will be full of light. But if your eye is bad, your whole body will be full of darkness."[1]

Both Marx and Jesus run the race to win. But head-on, they race in opposite directions.

*For defining of Marx's principles in context, see page 36.
**Engels, too, filled out Laura's questionnaire. For the character you most dislike, he wrote, "Spurgeon." Significantly, Spurgeon, a contemporary of Engels, was a popular Christian speaker/author. (Spurgeon's book is listed on back page.)

focus

In Marx's model state exists a vacuum central to his whole theory, writes Fritz Raddatz *(Karl Marx).* That vacuum is man. He is just an idea, a peg on which to hang hopes. Marx talks about "the people" or "the proletariat" and identifies the individual only in terms of his relationship to society.

"The history of all hitherto existing society is the history of class struggles," Marx begins his manifesto. He starts with society, with class warfare and death; then sets up battering rams to beat down the walls of capitalism. And with a call to armed revolution, he finishes. Communists can attain their ends only by the forcible overthrow of all existing social conditions, he contends. In his focus on the whole of society, he begins his manifesto with the bloody conflict between classes of people and ends with the same.

Jesus, in his manifesto, begins with a seed, a tiny, individual package of life in his hand. He came to bring life, he says.[2] He, in contrast to Marx, focuses on the individual. And as he begins his manifesto with individual responsibility, so he ends: He points to a time when each life will give a final accounting to him.

principles and predictions

Marx and Jesus differ in their attitudes toward power.

On his path to leadership, Marx with the backing of a faithful wife and an extraordinary friend stood up to other socialist leaders who vied with him for control of the communist movement. Marx won. He had the edge because after he and Engels wrote their manifesto, Marx knew the basic principles of his philosophy. Even though he had to adjust predictions, he kept his first objectives. On the foundation of public ownership of property achieved by violent overthrow of all existing social institutions, he stood his ground. With this clearcut and radical defining of communism and its goals, he could with confidence devise ways to eliminate his competition and consolidate his following.

In contrast to Marx's *modus operandi,* Jesus while on earth led as one humble before God and men. And he expects his followers to exhibit the same spirit. Whereas Marx vied for power, Jesus stood on the authority he knew he possessed. His confidence rested in the knowledge of his Father's backing. For this reason when he faced crucifixion, he saw resurrection on the other side. "All things have been delivered to me by my Father," he says. And after saying that, he promises his followers, "Come to me, all you who labor and are heavy laden, and I will give you rest. . . *for I am gentle and lowly in heart.*"[3] The satisfying rest he promises, he grounds in submission to authority.

Marx and Jesus differ in other ways, too. Although Marx for his time showed remarkable insight into the functioning and development of capitalism, his forecasts based on his foundational ideas failed to materialize. For example, he was right in these perceptions about capitalism: its absolute need for growth, technological progress, and innovation; the boom and bust of business cycles; the increase of hired employees and decrease of self-employed. But Marx was wrong about his foremost prognostication that communism would develop only in countries where capitalism has fully developed. Instead, the opposite is true: Communism rules in undeveloped countries—Russia, China, and the Third World. Moreover, Marx was wrong about the fate of the working class: Under capitalism conditions for the working class have not deteriorated as he predicted; rather, they have improved.

Also, the theories of Marx have not survived in the modern field of economics as even Marxist sympathizers admit. For one, John Gurley, economics professor at Stanford, says that if Marx returned today he'd find that modern economists support a philosophy he railed against. For they subscribe to the premise that ideas change the world. This contradicts Marx's theory that economic structuring determines ideas and all else that exists in society.

In contrast to Marx's failed predictions and theories, scripture records fulfillment of these most significant ones: Jesus' foretelling of betrayal; suffering under elders, chief priests, scribes in Jerusalem; his crucifixion; and his rising again on the third day. Upon the fulfillment of these prophecies hangs the expectations of Jesus' followers. And on these historical facts, Christians base their faith.

Marx and Jesus are similar in that neither one detailed what happens in the interim before the fruition of his kingdom (or society), which time still lies in the future. Marx didn't instruct beyond revolution. And

Jesus didn't even talk about the church as such. In fact, he used the word *church* only in passing in Matthew 16:18 and 18:17. (The word *church* means simply, *called out ones*.) As for practical social structuring, both men left that to a future follower—Marx to Lenin and Jesus to Paul.

Regarding the past, Marx said the bourgeois cannot see history in its true perspective because of the blinders of their economic class interests. And yet Marx implies he can lift himself *above* history. He doesn't, however, make the claim as does Jesus to lift himself *outside* of history into the eternal. "I and my Father are one,"[4] Jesus says. And "Before Abraham was, I AM."[5]

Broadly speaking Marx's message is *change the mode of production* whereas Jesus' theme is *change the heart*. Marx says a new society creates new men; Jesus says unless the hearts of men are made new, society cannot change. Furthermore, in his manifesto, Jesus says that no radical change for good will take place until he returns because he says that until that time, good and evil will co-exist.

ownership

Survivalists. That's how Marx depicts proletarians, or workers, under capitalism. He says they receive only enough wages to hold body and soul together; private ownership is the problem, he claims.

Marx's system of *public ownership* of all property, however, brings problems of its own. Thefts and misappropriations are inevitable, says Milovan Djilas *(The New Class)*. It's not just that poverty motivates people to steal "national property" but that Marxist property does not seem to belong to anyone. "All valuables are somehow rendered value-less," Djilas says.

Fritz J. Raddatz cites an early, still-revered socialist, Rosa Luxemburg, as the most profound critic of the defects in Marx's thinking and writing. Her critique is taboo in orthodox Marxist circles. She claims that Marx's analysis of the ownership of capital goes in a circle. Since only a small part of the accumulation of capital goes to the consumption of the capitalist, where does the surplus value go, she asks. It must go to consumers. How is it that *despite everything,* people in capitalist societies are better off, Luxemburg asks. About the society Marx envisions, she concludes, it "exists nowhere in the world of reality."

On the subject of capitalist ownership, Jesus dealt indirectly at least one time. In his parable of the vineyard, he told of a worker who grumbled because he received only a denarius for twelve hours' work while another received the same amount for only one hour's work. "Friend, I am not being unfair to you." the landowner told him. *"Didn't you agree to work for a denarius?* Take your pay and go. I want to give to the man who was hired last the same as I gave you. *Don't I have the right to do what I want with my own money? Or are you envious because I am generous?"*[6]

Putting aside the important spiritual interpretation, which doesn't apply to this question of ownership, consider what the landowner said: *"Didn't you agree to work for a denarius?"* Here Jesus upholds faithfulness to agreed-upon labor contracts. The landowner also said, *"Don't I have the right to do what I want with my own money?"* In this instance Jesus upholds private ownership and decision making about property owned. And lastly, the landowner said, *"Are you envious because I am generous?"* Generosity is an option he would not have without ownership.

morality

Though Marx in historical materialism declares the external world to be objective reality, he rejects the objective reality of absolute truth. Or he seems to. In actuality, what he disclaims is personal responsibility and morality according to bourgeois values, which values he equates with Christian morality. He sees Christian ideals as necessary to reinforce capitalist values but envisions a future free from what he calls superstitions of the past. For the discarded absolutes of the bourgeoisie, he replaces his own absolute, the primacy of the new "classless" society. In this ideal state, without religious crutches, the individual will have only the responsibility to uphold communist ideals. All other allegiances—such as to God, personal standards, family, or nation—Marx obliterates by the "higher" commitment to this new world society, which then becomes the new arbiter of standards. In this way, he establishes a new absolute base for morality, a collective base.

This new base combined with Marx's dialectics does strange things with the concept of morality. In Marx's theory of dialectic struggle, two

forces spiral in opposition until they merge into one new progression.
For example, bourgeoisie and proletariat merge to produce a classless
society. Stanford's John Gurley explains that according to the conflict
and resolution of dialectic thinking, "a thing or process is never simply
this or that; it is always both. . ."

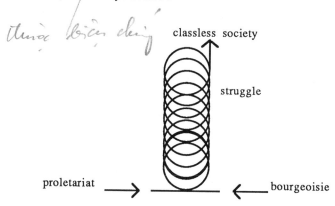

Figure 1: THE DIALECTIC PROCESS

    In the diagram, you can substitute another Marxist conflictual
process; for example, pagan religions in conflict with Christianity to
produce communism the result of progress, according to Marx's outlook. Or substitute *right* and *wrong* for the dialectic concepts in conflict
to produce a *new progression,* the final outcome. John Gurley explains
Marx's dialectic thinking by saying, "Right includes wrong and wrong
contains right." That's another way of saying that in this worldview,
there is no right or wrong, only historical progress.
    Isaiah Berlin in *Karl Marx,* expounds further. "The only sense in
which it is possible to show that something is good or bad, right or
wrong," he writes, is to demonstrate that it accords or discords with the
historical march toward communism. Today's communists in Latin
America say the same thing; they say that what lines up with revolution is moral and what does not is immoral.
    In contrast, concerning morality Jesus addresses the individual. His
focus is not on a historical process, a social movement, a theory, or an

abstraction but on a personal relationship with himself.

And this personal submission to himself includes submission to authority he institutes—from overall authority in government to the basic unit of society, the family. Within this basic unit, family responsibility includes sexual morality and respect for parental authority. Parental authority and responsibility, not children's rights, Jesus addresses primarily. "And you fathers," he admonishes, "do not provoke your children to wrath." For children, however, Jesus reserves one right in particular, the right to come to him. "Let the little children come to me and do not forbid them," he says. But Marx in the communist world's application of his atheistic principles denies children that access.

This submission to Jesus' instituted authority also entails individual accountability. Always to this end, Jesus focuses attention. In the Bible, every time a person complained to him about someone else, Jesus turned that one toward facing his own accountability. When a man told Jesus, "Tell my brother to divide the inheritance with me," Jesus refused to intervene. His answer was "Beware of covetousness." He told him life is more than accumulating property. Another one who complained was Martha. She claimed Mary, her sister, spent all her time sitting around listening to Jesus instead of helping her with the work. "Martha, Martha, you are worried and troubled about many things," Jesus said. "But one thing is needed, and Mary has chosen that good part, which will not be taken away from her." So far as we know, Jesus corrected Martha and said nothing to Mary.

The disciples, too, learned that complaining boomerangs. Because they had heard that Peter and John, through the petition of their mother, requested the highest positions in Jesus' future kingdom, they stewed. And this grumbling by the ten displeased Jesus. Whereas he hadn't rebuked Peter, John, or their mother for their request—he simply explained to them that his Father is the one who makes that decision— he called the ten in for a lesson in humility. Not prestige and power but the opportunity to serve[7]—that's what it's all about, Jesus told them.

In dealing with moral accountability, Jesus shifts the focus away from the accused and demands accountability from the accuser. "Judge not that you be not judged," he teaches.

social interaction and alienation

Although Marxism is a materialist philosophy, Marx cares not only about the economic status of man but also about his social status. Social relationship, in fact, is the centerpiece of his system. Marx accuses capitalism of centering on the commodity, which he labels a *fetish*. With this center, capitalists become pawns in the world they create for themselves, he says. And economic fetishism brings capitalists to their knees before *material* forces beyond their control, he adds. And yet, capitalists have the illusion, as masters of their work and its products, that they are organizing the world, Marx observes.

Only by human interaction, in fact, does Marx define the individual: He calls man an "ensemble of social relationships." For the disruption of this human relatedness, he blames capitalism because specialized jobs separate man from the product he makes. In the capitalistic process, he says the worker becomes an appendage to a machine, not an artisan of a craft. Marx says this separation of the worker from his creation causes a sense of *alienation* because, unlike in primeval barter of goods, the laborer loses his consciousness of social involvement.

Irrespective of the economic or political system, Jesus also deals with the alienation problem. But he speaks not of alienation from things or people. He sees man's central problem as his alienation from God by sin. For this Jesus came to bridge the gap. Those so reconciled by him enter into relationship with his living body, the church, and interact in a new way with the world.

freedom

The concept of freedom, a uniquely human necessity, differs under communism. A capitalist democracy says a citizen may do all except what law prohibits, but communism says he can do only what the state allows. The party can punish arbitrarily for "the interest of the state" or "the interest of the party." And because of this, even if the constitution and laws guarantee freedom, the communist application of this concept negates promised liberty according to the dictate of the leadership.

Marx admits capitalism offers freedom. He recognizes that under capitalism a laborer is free to choose or quit employment. Nevertheless, he belittles the bourgeois concept of liberty. The worker, he says, receives only partial payment for labor he sells like a commodity; in selling his labor, he has to compete with fellow laborers; and he submits to alienation from the creation of his labor—all of this to capitalist advantage. Without economic freedom, Marx claims, a worker is not free.

Freedom is one of many terms Marx redefines. The freedom he promises is not just "freedom from" or even "right to do," but the freedom "to have the material means to do." In Marx's ideology, freedom comes only with collective ownership of the means of production.

In saying that freedom is more than "freedom from," Marx gives the impression that he expands the outer limits of freedom and, hence, offers more than the capitalism he spurns. But while holding out with one hand the never-attained goal of egalitarianism, or equality of results, he takes away with the other hand all private ownership. Then he centralizes *all* power—political, economic, social—in clay-footed guardians, human beings. And that is the point of weakness in Marx's system. Noted journalist Walter Lippmann points out the danger of this kind of power. He warns that to forget long ages of suffering caused by man's dominion over man is to forget that unlimited power, exercised by limited man, can lead only to oppression and corruption.

With power thus entrusted and incentive for production destroyed by methods of force, the practice of freedom does not match the promise of Marx's theory. The reason for this failure is that Marx promises the unattainable: *equality of results.* On the other hand, marketplace capitalism, which Marx attacks, offers the attainable: *equality of opportunity.* It depends for its results, not on the innate goodwill of the citizenry or their leaders, but on the measure of the individual's own efforts and voluntary association. Also, democratic capitalism's multiple ownership of property by many individuals diffuses power.

The difference in the two systems is even more basic. Objectivist philosopher Ayn Rand explains that in collectivism men's lives belong to society. To submit to this system—whether by idealistic choice, by default, or by force or intimidation—citizens must be willing to give over their personal freedoms for the collectivist variety. That premise, once accepted, gives the state the right to organize the lives of its members, to set their goals, and to distribute their goods.

Even Marx admits that before full communism is achieved, despotism may be necessary. This he justifies by charging the bourgeoisie with exploitation. This stage of confiscation of property and the liquidation of the bourgeoisie he looks upon as a necessary and temporary measure. Therefore, until class struggle subsides and government withers away, the countries we Americans call communist call themselves socialist and on the road to communism, or a classless society. Unfortunately their ideal, like a mirage, remains one step ahead all the time. The Soviet Union after seventy years does not claim to have attained communism. It is still socialist and still under a dictatorship.

The kind of freedom Jesus offers is different. He says he offers freedom from the degradation of sin and its consequence, death; and even freedom from bondage to his own Father's moral code, by virtue of his fulfillment of that law in himself and through him in the lives of believers. He offers not just the "freedom from" of capitalism or the "freedom to have the means to do" of Marxism but promises "freedom to be" what the human heart longs for and what God intends: "Where the Spirit of the Lord is, there is liberty. But we all, with unveiled face, beholding as in a mirror the glory of the Lord, are being transformed into the same image."[8]

This freedom can be abdicated but cannot be stolen. That's what the Bible implies when it says,"Stand fast therefore in the liberty by which Christ has made us free."[9] The Bible also says this kind of freedom fulfills: It speaks of "the perfect law of liberty."[10] And finally, it says, in the end after the final judgment, this freedom will be universal: "The creation itself also will be delivered from the bondage of corruption."[11] That's hard to top.

PART B
MARX

Never can I be at peace,
For my soul is powerfully driven,
I must strive and struggle onward
In a restless fury of my own.

I would conquer everything there is,
All the loveliest graces of the gods,
Embracing all the wisdom of the world,
And all the arts and songs.

—Karl Marx
Book of Love
(written in his youth)

from "Never can I be at peace", Franz Mehring,
aus dem literarischen Nachlass, I, p. 28
Marx, Robert Payne

his life

MARX

Karl Marx was different.

His parents knew it. Others saw it.

And Marx, like Walt Whitman, celebrated himself.

History paints the picture of a man on his way: If he couldn't walk through a path yielded to him, he elbowed through the political crowd.

Marx's friends and foes agree on the forcefulness of his personality. Some call him arrogant; others are more charitable in their descriptions. Karl Kautsky, a German journalist, said Marx had a "mighty personality which overpowered at the same time as it enchanted."

Another contemporary colleague, Paul Annenkov, describes Marx: He is "made up of energy, will power and unshakable conviction, a type that is highly remarkable even at first glance. . . His coat buttoned awry, he nevertheless gave the appearance of a man who has the right and the power to command attention, however odd his appearance and his actions might seem. His movements were awkward but bold and self-confident. . . his words were sharpened by what seemed to me an almost painful tone which rang through everything that he said. This tone expressed a firm conviction that it was his mission to dominate other minds and prescribe laws for them."

Intimate family friend Wilhelm Liebknecht saw Marx this way: "He had a gift for inspiring confidence. . . As a teacher Marx had the rare quality of being severe without discouraging. . . No one could be kinder and fairer than Marx in giving others their due."

Marx described himself and his followers more severely. In his 1849 Cologne newspaper when he knew he was to be expelled from Prussia, he wrote, "We are ruthless and we ask no quarter from you. When our turn comes, we shall not disguise our terrorism."

his youth

On May 5, 1818, Karl Marx was born in Trier or Treves, the west-ernmost town in central Germany, at that time called Prussia. It had Catholic cathedrals, ancient Roman ruins, and twelve thousand citizens.

Both of Karl's parents came from rabbinical families; his father, Herschel Marx, came from a line of rabbis dating back to the 1500s, but Karl's father broke from that tradition. Because Prussian laws banned Jews from state service, Herschel joined the protestant church to continue practicing law. Before that time, influenced by the Enlighten-ment era, he had already abandoned his Jewish faith. Now he also took a Christian name, Heinrich, and sent Karl to a protestant school.

Upon graduation from secondary school, Karl had to write an essay on religion, in which he explained the fall of man, his consequent sep-aration from God by sin, and the restoration of that broken relationship by forgiveness through the Redeemer. Marx understood the gospel.

Thus Karl Marx was a Jew but not a Jew, a Christian but not a Christian, a Prussian but not a Prussian—not a Prussian because he renounced his citizenship to become a world citizen and later an exile. Contradictions like these were part of the personal life of Marx; and later his theory of contradictions became a key principle of dialectics.

A great influence on Karl as a boy was a neighboring baron, Ludwig von Westphalen. The gentleman gave him access to his library and, on their long walks together, discussed with him Shakespeare, Homer, and world literature. After a year in college, eighteen year old Marx became engaged to this man's daughter Jenny. She was twenty-two.

Then, back in college for his second year, Karl forsook his formal studies for independent reading and poetry writing and caused his father concern. In a letter about Karl's engagement to Jenny, his father ex-presses genuine love. "If after serious self-examination you really per-sist in this view, then you must become a man at once," Heinrich Marx wrote. "You know, my dear Karl, that for love of you I have agreed to something that is not really in keeping with my character and from time to time it certainly gives me anxiety. . . I cannot and will not conceal my weakness towards you. Sometimes my heart revels in thoughts of you and your future. And yet sometimes I cannot drive away sad, ominous, fearful ideas when the thought suddenly creeps in: Does your heart match your head and your abilities? Does your heart really have room for the earthly but gentler feelings, which are so very comforting to Man in this Vale of sorrows? And, since your heart is clearly enlivened and governed by a spirit that is not given to all men, I ask whether this spirit is of a heavenly or a Faustian Nature? Do you think—and this is not the least painful of my doubts—that you will ever be capable of feeling a truly human, a domestic happiness?. . . Although I love you more than anything. . . I am not blind. . . I cannot quite get rid of the idea that you are not free from egoism, that you have more of it than one needs for self-preservation. . . But for your own sake I shall never stop lecturing you until I am convinced that this blemish has gone from your otherwise noble character. . ."

"Only if your heart remains pure and beats like a man's," Karl's father continues, "only if no demonic spirit has the power to alienate your heart from better feelings—only then shall I find the happiness that for years I have been dreaming I might find through you; else I should see the finest goal of my life destroyed." The father wanted his son to prepare for the future, but he found no comfort in Karl's answer.

The first year, when Karl was at the Bonn, Heinrich had paid his son's debts, but the next year at the University in Berlin, Heinrich scolded him for extravagance: "Just as if we were made of money, Your Highness has gone through almost 700 taler. . . whereas the very richest do not spend 500." In the year Heinrich Marx wrote this, he died.

Several years later, with special study of the philosophy of Hegel, Marx received a doctorate. Though Hegel exalted a divine being, Marx and his fellow "Young Hegelians" saw only what they wanted to see—godless revolutionary justification in the theology. Marx called this reversal "setting Hegel on his head."

Upon graduation, because of his anti-God view, Marx was unable to secure a university position; so he found employment with a Cologne newspaper. But once again he was in trouble. Because Marx criticized the Russian government, the Prince of Prussia acceded to the Russian Czar's request to have him fired from his job. Therefore, at the age of twenty-five, Marx was unemployed and back in his hometown Trier.

formative days

In the future Marx was seldom to be gainfully employed because pursuing a career was not the driving force of his life. From his college days to the time of co-authoring the famous *Communist Manifesto,* this man with the commanding air sought as though driven to unlock the mystery of destiny for the world and for himself.

In this pursuit of his own credo, Marx had to have input from others. Hegel was one of many from whose ideas he borrowed. From this most influential philosopher in his time, Marx gleaned dialectics, one of his most important principles, the premise that progress comes only through class conflict. Then, with other Young Hegelians, Marx discarded the miraculous and supernatural of Hegel to replace them with a materialist view of the world. From there he moved on with the teachings of Ludwig Feuerbach to establish himself as an atheist.

But unlike other Young Hegelians, Marx wasn't satisfied just with dethroning God and opposing the religious establishment. He wanted to apply his theories. This led to a desire to incorporate his ideas into a political program; socialists attracted him. One of them, Saint Simon, led him to search through history to study cause and effect. Until this time, Marx had listened to Professor Bruno Bauer and his brother, who claimed that ideas shape history. But after much investigation, Marx shook loose from the concept that ideas are the springboard from which all else derives. Instead he concluded that history shapes ideas. In that case, events in history mold men's beliefs and create their institutions, not the reverse. If so, why not cooperate with the direction not fight against it, Marx reasoned. With this, he made another breakthrough!

Marx, one of many in a milieu of social ferment, a time of restless discontent, continued to ask questions and to fit answers into the framework he was building. From Moses Hess, he learned about the interplay of social forces in revolution. From Saint-Simon, again, he learned that economic forces determine history. From Proudhon, he learned about the nature of property. "Property is theft," Proudhon wrote. From the poet Heinrich Heine, he learned of conflict between *haves* and *have-nots.* From Eduard Gans, Weitling, and Blanqui, he came to recognize the importance of the proletariat, or working class, in industrial society.

For developing a unified system upon which to hang his ideology, Marx was indebted not to his native German theorists but to English economists: Locke, Adam Smith, Ricardo and others. Smith and Ricardo said the price of a commodity reflects labor time; Marx in his labor theory of value expands that to say labor power itself is a commodity.

These economists operate in a materialist realm of things measurable. From them Marx took the tag of "science" even though he couldn't verify his findings. He interpreted rather than measured or described; and lacking hard evidence, he culled the "essence." Without knowing it, Marx broke ground in a new field, the socio-analysis of economics.

During this time, Marx was engaged to Jenny von Westphalen for seven years. Now with a promise of a journalism job in Paris, he married his hometown sweetheart. Marx was proud of his wife's beauty, her birth, and her intelligence and "leaned on her unhesitatingly in all times of crisis and disaster," Isaiah Berlin writes.

his goal fixed

In Paris in 1844, knowing the full import and danger of the political package he had been assembling, Marx came to the point of commitment. It happened when he met with Friedrich Engels for their first serious exchange of ideas. The chemistry of that encounter enabled him to accept, not invent, an explosive, international label. The decision to wear this tag set the course of his life: He became a "communist." Though Marx did not begin the communist movement nor create its name, he now moved himself forward to set his hand to its helm.

And also in Paris Marx began the most important association of his life, besides his marriage: his friendship with Friedrich Engels. Engels was to become the single, largest source of financial support for Marx and his family. Even more important was to be his role as confidant, moral supporter, idea man, ramrod, and writing collaborator.

But Marx's days in Paris were numbered. On 1 February 1845, because of pressure from the Prussian government, France forced Marx to leave Paris to go to Brussels, Belgium. There in spring 1845, Engels wrote that Marx laid out before him the materialist interpretation of history that accredits economy to be the root from which all else grows.

In January 1848 for the Communist League, Marx and Engels deliv-

ered to the printer the *Communist Manifesto,* their greatest collaboration. For this relatively small organization, the two men expressed
vision more than reality at the time. Boldly they spoke out: "A specter
is haunting Europe—the specter of communism. . . Communism is
already acknowledged by all European powers to be itself a power." And
the finale: "The communists disdain to conceal their views and aims.
They openly declare that their ends can be attained only by the forcible
overthrow of all existing social conditions. Let the ruling classes tremble at a communistic revolution."

The *Communist Manifesto*—except for the outdated third section on
socialist literature—even for today's reader is interesting, readable, clear,
and has a touch of humor. Soon after its publication on 23 February
1848, Belgium expelled Marx. On 24 February revolution broke out in
France. Then, after a brief time in Paris, the Marx family went back to
Cologne, Germany on 15 March and began a new newspaper.

In Germany, the bourgeoisie still struggled for ascendancy over the
aristocracy. And because time was not ripe there for the proletariat to
rise up, Marx pushed for a bourgeois revolution. Since he did not promote a working class revolution, Marx enraged members of the Communist League. And how did Marx meet this opposition? In the way
he'd overcome opposition in the future: He dissolved the group.

With that opposition out of the way, Marx sought the support of
the German bourgeois, who suspected him of a proletarian bent. Marx's
solution this time? Employing another tactic he would use again in the
future, he formed an alliance. In this case, he sought to save his newspaper by joining hands with resisters who refused to pay taxes.

Though the alliance succeeded, the action led to his arrest. By his
own defense, however, he won his case with the jury. Notwithstanding,
once again he had to leave his German homeland.

in exile in England

Marx was now thirty years old.

When Marx and his family set out for London in 1849, they did not
know they would spend the rest of their lives there. Nor did they foresee
that for twenty years the growing family and the servant provided by
Jenny's family would live a poverty stricken life.

For this hardship Karl and Jenny were not prepared by their upbringing and heritage. Like Karl, Johanna Bertha Julie Jenny Marx—Jenny Marx's full name—had grown up in comfort amounting to luxury. Nevertheless, for herself she could accept privation because she entered marriage committed both to revolution and to her husband. But in a letter to a friend, she expressed misgivings about her children having no religious identity: "They have been brought up with notions and views that form a complete barrier to the society in which they move. . . It is hardly the right thing to bring them up in harsh disagreement with society. . . these matters weigh heavily upon me."

Could it be that she regretted forsaking her Scottish Presbyterian background? A look at her maternal family tree reveals two ministers and the daughter of a minister. Jenny probably did not discard all her past, however; she may have been the one to establish the Marx family tradition of celebrating Christmas.

In spite of societal pressure, the daughters remained true to their irreligious upbringing. Daughter Jenny later, as pictures show, wore a cross—but only to honor the European Catholic struggle, she claimed. Another daughter Eleanor later in life became proud of her Jewish heritage and proclaimed her ethnicity—but not her faith—as a Jewess.

In other ways, too, the family felt society's pressure. The parents felt they had to keep up bourgeois appearances. When visitors came, Jenny, for the occasion, would retrieve from the pawnshops the necessary silver and china. Also, in the family's greatest destitution, the parents provided bourgeois culture for their daughters—music and language lessons.

Sundays Marx often reserved for outings with his family. And on weekdays, he allowed his children to interrupt his work. Although he usually studied at the British Museum, sometimes he wrote at home. There the children diverted his attention with such games as lining up their chairs behind his chair to make a train. His gentleness with them contrasted sharply with his political personality.

But all was not happy romps in the Marx household. "Marx was never one to balance his books," writes Robert Heilbroner, Marxist scholar and a Norman Thomas Professor of Economics. "Had Marx bccn a financially ordcrly pcrson," hc says, "thc family might havc lived in decency." Instead they lived from one financial crisis to another.

During their poverty, family members alternated periods of ill health. Marx himself often suffered from boils and carbuncles. Also, three children died, two in infancy and a beloved son at the age of nine. Of four daughters and two sons, only three daughters lived to adulthood.

Toward his three daughters Marx was protective in a traditional way in spite of his otherwise liberal views. In a letter to Paul Lafargue, his daughter Laura's suitor, Marx questions the young man's economic preparedness for marriage. "You know," he writes, "that I have sacrificed my whole fortune to the revolutionary struggle. I do not regret it. On the contrary. Had I my career to start again, I should do the same. But I would not marry. As far as lies in my power I intend to save my daughter from the reefs on which her mother's life has been wrecked."

In contrast to advocating free love in his manifesto, Marx warns Lefargue against "too intimate deportment." "To my mind, true love expresses itself in the lover's restraint, modest bearing, even diffidence regarding the adored one, and certainly not in unconstrained passion and manifestations of premature familiarity," he writes. And he warns Lafargue to listen or he may have to love Laura from a distance. Later Lafargue married Laura and became Marx's assistant.

Of Marx's three children who lived to adulthood, all the daughters were named Jenny after their mother, but only one was called Jenny. Unfortunately, the lives of all three ended in tragedy. In January 1883, Jenny at age thirty-eight died after her mother's death on 2 December 1881 and before the death of her grief stricken father, who died on 14 March 1883. Another daughter, Eleanor, took poison in her early forties. And daughter Laura committed suicide in 1911.

In England, besides revolutionary work, Marx spent most of his time studying and writing. His most monumental work was *Capital,* of which he completed only the first of three volumes. Through it, he hoped to reveal the future collapse of capitalism and also to reap the book's profits. During his life, however, the book did not sell well.

By now a pattern emerges in Marx's life. He learned from others. Then when these same ones opposed him, he set his mind to deposing each one. In revolutionary groups, Marx first positioned himself to write their charters, then positioned himself to dominate the groups, first the Communist League and then the International Working Men's Association. But later he had controversies with rival leaders Lassalle, Proudhon, and Bakunin. In his failure to keep control, Marx fell back on the strategy that if a group heads the wrong direction, dissolve it. That's what he did to both groups.

Moses Hess, the one who introduced Engels to communism, said, "It is a pity, a terrible pity that [Marx], who is easily the most gifted member of our Party. . . seems to demand a kind of personal submission which I for one will never concede to any man." This same editor years earlier in 1841 in Cologne had hailed twenty-three year old Marx as "perhaps the only real philosopher now living. . . a sort of Rousseau, Voltaire, Holbach, Lessing, Heine, and Hegel rolled into one."

Gustav Techow, a Prussian revolutionary, also grieved over the world's loss in this talented man: "[Marx] gave the impression not only of rare intellectual superiority but also of outstanding personality. If he had as much heart as intellect and love as hate, I should have gone through fire for him. . . I regret that this man, with his fine intellect, is lacking in nobility of soul. I am convinced that the most dangerous ambition has eaten away all the good in him."

his legacy

To know the life and character of Marx is to understand his legacy. "The Marxist tradition, like the Christian tradition, is not only a matter of doctrine—it is a matter also of the imitation of the Master," writes J. Hampden Jackson in *Marx, Proudhon and European Socialism.* He explains further: "What persisted among communists was the [temperament] as well as the teaching of Marx. The vindictive hatred with which Karl Marx had pursued every colleague who was not an obedient disciple was copied in every communist regime. The authoritarianism and intolerance which had been characteristic of Marx himself continued to characterize the party and governmental officials who were to act in his name."

Jackson concludes with this: "It could all have been predicted."

chapter three—MARX: his manifesto, chart two

INTRODUCTORY AID TO MARX'S MANIFESTO*

At the time Marx and Engels wrote this manifesto in Germany, though claiming to speak for world communism, they were in reality speaking for a small Communist League in London. But Marx thought in universal terms. With his introduction he lays down the gauntlet before the bourgeoisie and stakes out his claims for the future of the world's proletariats.

section by section summaries of Marx's ideas

1. bourgeois and proletarians

In this section Marx traces his view of history in terms of struggle between oppressed and oppressing classes. He outlines economic stages of development, seeking to prove that the structure of the economy is the foundation upon which everything in society builds—philosophy, religion, social institutions, customs. He claims that the ruling class of any age sets the rules. He lists historical progression: After the aristocracy came a highly stratified society under feudalism with a conflict between classes seeking supremacy. From that emerged as victor the bourgeoisie, who spawned, for their selfish purposes, the proletariat. The rising of each new class brought progress but also more conflict. With these last last two classes heading for a final showdown, the bourgeoisie simultaneously oppress and train up the proletariat. And thus, they dig their own graves.

*For convenience, the Communist Manifesto will be called Marx's manifesto hereafter.

2. proletarians and communists

Here Marx claims that the communist party is spokesman for the proletariat, or working class, everywhere. The communist aim, he says, is to abolish private property. He anticipates the outcries of the bourgeoisie at communist proposals and bluntly ridicules their complaints one by one.

3. socialist and communist literature (outdated section)

Marx reviews the literature of contemporary socialists of various stripes, listing wherein they fall short of revolution, the goal of the Communist Party. Not only are these others doomed to failure, but they are a drag on progress, he says.

4. position of the communists in relation to the various existing opposition parties

Marx lists those groups with which he allies himself. He does not have to support a group's ideas to support them in their cause just so long as they are moving in the direction he sees history moving. In other words, he supports every revolutionary movement.

First and foremost Marx lays out the priority of instilling in the working class an awareness of the antagonism between the bourgeoisie and the proletariat. And he always keeps before everyone the leading question about property ownership.

Watch out, you ruling classes, says Marx, because, ready or not, here we come.

MARX: his manifesto, chart three **I. BOURGEOIS AND PROLETARIANS**

READING AID: Overview, Section I,
the Manifesto of the Communist Party

Middle arrows flow from
both top and bottom

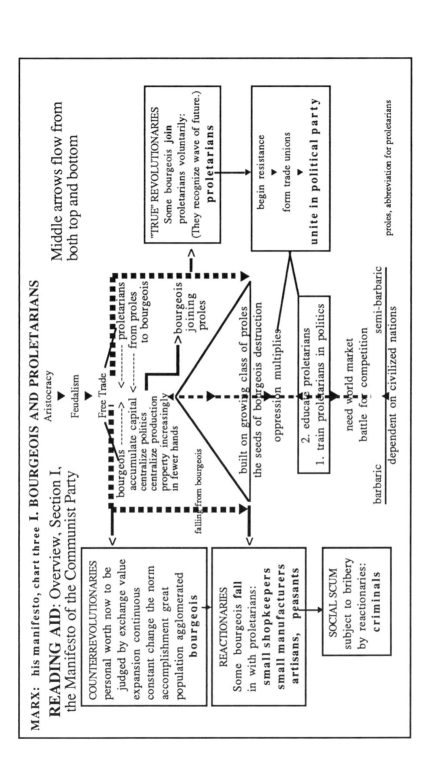

"TRUE" REVOLUTIONARIES
Some bourgeois **join**
proletarians voluntarily:
(They recognize wave of future.)
proletarians

begin resistance
▼
form trade unions
▼
unite in political party

Aristocracy
▼
Feudalism

Free Trade

proletarians
<----- from proles
<----- to bourgeois

bourgeois ------->
accumulate capital
centralize politics
centralize production
property increasingly
in fewer hands

>bourgeois
joining
proles

falling from bourgeois

built on growing class of proles
the seeds of bourgeois destruction
oppression multiplies

2. educate proletarians
1. train proletarians in politics

need world market
battle for competition

semi-barbaric
barbaric
dependent on civilized nations

proles, abbreviation for proletarians

COUNTERREVOLUTIONARIES
personal worth now to be
judged by exchange value
expansion continuous
constant change the norm
accomplishment great
population agglomerated
bourgeois

REACTIONARIES
Some bourgeois **fall**
in with proletarians:
**small shopkeepers
small manufacturers
artisans, peasants**

SOCIAL SCUM
subject to bribery
by reactionaries:
criminals

MARX: his manifesto, chart four

I. PROLETARIANS AND COMMUNISTS: Summary of points MARX makes in Section II of his manifesto

Distinguishing feature of communism: abolition of private property. Capital becomes common property of all members of society.

Property does not become social property: It is already social property. What changes is its class character; it loses its bourgeois character.

Bourgeoisie: Living labor is means to accumulate capital for bourgeois. Communists: Living labor is means to enrich laborers, or proletarians.

Communism differs from other working class parties in two ways:
1. Communists point out common ties, independent of nationality.
2. Communists represent the movement as a whole.

By revolution, communism . . . .
▌ will wrest, even by "despotic" means, all capital from the bourgeois,
▌ will centralize in the state all instruments of production,
▌ will thus sweep away conditions that produce class antagonism,
▌ will develop each person to guarantee the free development of all.

probable measures necessary to begin proletarian rule in advanced countries

▌ Abolition of ownership of land; appropriation of rents of land for public purposes
▌ A heavy, graduated income tax
▌ Abolition of all right of inheritance
▌ Confiscation of property of emigrants and rebels
▌ Centralization of credit in the state—a national bank with state capital and exclusive monopoly
▌ Centralization in state: communication and transport
▌ Increase in factories and instruments of production owned by the state; cultivation of waste land
▌ Equal liability of all to labor: establishment of industrial & farming armies
▌ Combination of agriculture and manufacturing; abolition of distinction between town and country by distribution of population
▌ Free universal public education

MARX: his manifesto, chart five

READING AID for Marx's manifesto: summary of Marx's arguments against bourgeois accusations

bourgeois accusations

1. You abolish private property.

2. You abolish culture.

3. You abolish the family. We shudder!
4. You stop exploitation of children by parents.
5. You replace home education with social.
6. You introduce free love
7. You abolish countries and national lines.
8. You abolish religion, morality, eternal truths.

Communist (proletarian) answers

1. You eliminate private property for nine-tenths of the people.
   We allow it, but do not allow any to subjugate the labor of others.
2. *What* culture? The culture that trains workers to act as a machine?
   You share the illusions of ruling classes before you.
3. You deny family ties to proletarians whose children labor for you.
4. We plead guilty.
5. We rescue education from your rule.
6. We eliminate your hypocrisy and private and public prostitution.
7. We eliminate not only class antagonisms but also national ones.
8. You're right! We explode myths.

Marx's theoretical principles
terms defined in context
capitalism

Marx explains that the capitalist accumulates capital by paying the laborer only enough for survival and using the rest, or *surplus value,*[1] for himself for personal income, or *revenue,*[2] for land rent and interest, and for investment and reinvestment, or *capital.*[3] Under capitalism, *relations of production*[4] (social arrangements) are exploitive, Marx says. He bases his conclusion on the assumption that *"capital*[3] is stored-up labor."* Marx reasons that whereas labor in the act of production is *living labor,*[5] labor stored up in machines is *dead labor.*[6] Hence the wealth a capitalist receives really belongs to hired labor, Marx concludes.

This "labor-produced" capital the owner uses to pay for the *means of production*[7] (raw materials, equipment). Then this means of production together with hired labor produces a *commodity*,[8] which the owner can sell at a higher price than the value he invested. The price that the market supports is called the *exchange value*[9] of the commodity; in primitive tribal communism, only *use value*[10] has meaning. Likewise, in modern communism—unless the government has introduced market practices—*use value*,[10] not *exchange value*,[9] is primary.

Not only do capitalists not dictate history, Marx says, they set the stage for their own overthrow. In order to outdo competitors, the *bourgeois*[11] build up the *proletarians*[12] by training them in skills and political know-how. By capitalists thus contributing to workers' growth in expertise and numbers, they also contribute to the workers' consciousness of class, discontent, and solidarity. And in this way, the bourgeois capitalists endanger their own positions.

communism

Communism will replace capitalism to become the new *mode of production* [13] Marx says. And it will produce new social arrangements, which Marx calls new *relations of production*.[4] These reorganized work units will direct the work of the population, the use of their skills, the arts, techniques, and distribution of products, all of which Marx calls the *forces of production*.[14] The people will now own the raw materials, auxiliary materials, and the *instruments of labor*[15] (tools, machinery, etc.), the combination of which Marx calls the *means of production.*[7]

In communism, no longer will the worker be separated from his product by *the division of labor*[16] as in the capitalist *mode of production*.[13] Although society will not return to primitive communism—that is, tribal life in which each individual supplies his own needs—society will enter a new phase of communal ownership and enterprise, in which all will contribute to the larger tasks of modern society, and all will receive equally in return; in other words, the economy will be a *socialized* one.[17]

class struggle

Through history Marx traces *class struggle*,[18] or conflict between economic classes. Out of each struggle comes a new, better social arrangement. He calls this spiral progress of rising out of itself to a higher plane *dialectic process*[19]. In the past this process has been the history of the ruling class accumulating wealth at the expense of another class or classes, he says. Although he gives recognition to the accomplishments of each ruling class, he portrays them as traveling the road to their own destruction and blames them for prevailing poverty and injustice.

According to Marx's interpretation, out of the present day rule of the bourgeoisie over the proletariat will emerge a worldwide *classless society*[20] composed of *new men.*[21] (Modern day Marxists name this conflictual process *dialectic materialism*.)[22] All classes before the *proletariat*[23] had a status quo to preserve, but this one does not. With the proletariat's annihilation of the bourgeoisie, society will be classless and will offer equality for all. Marx calls this *egalitarianism*.[24]

history, a new view
This principle of dialectics Marx incorporates into his philosophic view of history based on materialism. *Materialism*[25] stands in opposition to idealism, as illustrated in the following: A tree falls in the forest. CRASH! The earth vibrates. Noise fills the airwaves. The age-old question is if no one is present to hear the noise, is the noise real?

Idealism[26] in philosophy as defined by the academic world says, no—that sound is sound only when someone is present to hear it. It argues that reality exists only in the perceptions and ideas of man, in subjective apprehension. But *materialism*[25] says, yes: Noise is noise whether anyone hears it or not; physical matter—even sound traveling on airwaves—is the objective and ultimate reality of the universe.

Marx endorses materialism but gives the traditional concept of materialism a different twist. For him history is not the story of external influences affecting man or even the story of man's interaction with his own institutions. It's the story of man gaining control of the natural world, not by contemplation or knowledge as ancient Aristotle and others propose, but by labor. *Man acts on his environment and in so doing, he creates himself.*

In China, if you ask someone who created him, he will answer "labor." Trofim Lysenko clarifies the communist attitude: "In our Soviet Union people are not born. What are born are organisms. We turn them into people—tractor drivers, engine drivers, academicians, scholars, and so forth."

At times Marx's approach to history seems to be *deterministic*[27] or fatalistic, but at other times he warns against using historical materialism in a *mechanical and undialectic*[28] way. Friedrich Engels best sums up Marx's historical method in his speech at the graveside of his best friend and collaborator. "Just as Darwin discovered the law of development of organic nature," Engels told the bereaved, "so Marx discovered the law of development of human history." Engels pointed out that Marx says "mankind must first of all eat, drink, have shelter and clothing, before it can pursue politics, science, art, religion." He also stated that Marx explains history a new way—not as a result of the influence of art, institutions, or religion. Engels said Marx claims economics to be the foundation upon which state institutions, law, art, and even religion evolves. Marx says the economy is the foundation from which all else derives.

MARX'S INTRODUCTION TO
THE MANIFESTO OF THE COMMUNIST PARTY

A specter is haunting Europe--the specter of communism. All the powers of old Europe have entered into a holy alliance to exorcise this specter; Pope and Czar, Metternich and Guizot, French radicals, and German police spies.

Where is the party in opposition that has not been decried as communistic by its opponents in power? Where the opposition that has not hurled back the branding reproach of communism against the more advanced opposition parties, as well as against its reactionary adversaries?

Two things result from this fact.

I. Communism is already acknowledged by all European powers to be itself a power.

II. It is high time that communists should openly, in the face of the whole world, publish their views, their aims, their tendencies, and meet this nursery tale of the specter of communism with a manifesto of the party itself.

To this end, communists of various nationalities have assembled in London and sketched the following manifesto, to be published in the English, French, German, Italian, Flemish, and Danish languages.

Friedrich Engels in his 1888 preface wrote, "The manifesto has become a historical document which we have no longer any right to alter. The present translation is by Mr. Samuel Moore, the translator of the greater portion of Marx's "Capital." We have revised it in common, and I have added a few notes explanatory of historical allusions."

THE MANIFESTO OF MARX (and Engels)

TEXT OF THE COMMUNIST MANIFESTO

1 - BOURGEOIS AND PROLETARIANS*

The history of all hitherto existing society** is the history of class struggles.

Freeman and slave, patrician and plebian, lord and serf, guildmaster,+ and journeyman, in a word, oppressor and oppressed, stood in constant opposition to one another, carried on uninterrupted, now hidden, now open fight, a fight that each time ended, either in a revolutionary reconstitution of society at large, or in the common ruin of the contending classes.

In the earlier epochs of history we find almost everywhere a complicated arrangement of society into various orders, a manifold gradation of social rank. In ancient Rome we have patricians, knights, plebeians, slaves; in the middle ages, feudal lords, vassals, guildmasters, journeymen, apprentices, serfs; in almost all of these classes, again, subordinate gradations.

The modern bourgeois society that has sprouted from the ruins of feudal society, has not done away with class antagonisms. It has but esta-

---

*By bourgeosie is meant the class of modern capitalists, owners of the means of social production and employers of wage labor. By proletariat, the class of modern wage laborers who, having no means of production of their own, are reduced to selling their labor power in order to live.

**That is, all written history. In 1847, the prehistory of society, the social organization existing previous to recorded history, was all but unknown. Since then Haxthausen discovered common ownership of land in Russia, Maurer proved it to be the social foundation from which all Teutonic races started in history, and bye and bye village communities were found to be, or to have been, the primitive form of society everywhere from India to Ireland. The inner organization of this primitive communistic society was laid bare, in its typical form, by Morgan's crowning discovery of the true nature of the *gens* and its relation to the *tribe*. With the dissolution of these primeval communities society begins to be differentiated into separate and finally antagonistic classes. I have attempted to retrace this process of dissolution in: "Der Ursprung der Familie, des Privateigenthums und des Staats," 2nd edit., Stuttgart, 1886.

+Guildmaster, that is, a full member of a guild, a master within, not a head.

blished new classes, new conditions of oppression, new forms of struggle in place of the old ones.

Our epoch, the epoch of the bourgeoisie, possesses, however, this distinctive feature; it has simplified the class antagonisms. Society as a whole is more and more splitting up into two great hostile camps, into two great classes directly facing each other: Bourgeoisie and Proletariat.

From the serfs of the middle ages sprang the chartered burghers of the earliest towns. From these burgesses the first elements of the bourgeoisie were developed.

The discovery of America, the rounding of the Cape, opened up fresh ground for the rising bourgeoisie. The East Indian and Chinese markets, the colonization of America, trade with the colonies, the increase in the means of exchange and in commodities generally, gave to commerce, to navigation, to industry, an impulse never before known, and thereby, to the revolutionary element in the tottering feudal society, a rapid development.

The feudal system of industry, under which industrial production was monopolized by closed guilds, now no longer sufficed for the growing wants of the new market. The manufacturing system took its place. The guildmasters were pushed on one side by the manufacturing middle class: division of labor between the different corporate guilds vanished in the face of division of labor in each single workshop.

Meantime the markets kept ever growing, the demand ever rising. Even manufacture no long sufficed. Thereupon, steam and machinery revolutionized industrial production. The place of manufacture was taken by the giant, modern industry, the place of the industrial middle class, by industrial millionaires, the leaders of whole industrial armies, the modern bourgeois.

Modern industry has established the world market, for which the discovery of America paved the way. This market has given immense development to commerce, to navigation, to communication by land. This development has, in its turn, reacted on the extension of industry; and in proportion as industry, commerce, navigation, railways extended, in the same proportion the bourgeoisie developed, increased its capital, and pushed into the background every class handed down from the Middle Ages.

We see, therefore, how the modern bourgeoisie is itself the product of a long course of development, of a series of revolutions in the modes of production and of exchange.

Each step in the development of the bourgeoisie was accompanied by a corresponding political advance of that class. An oppressed class under the sway of the feudal nobility, an armed and self-governing association in the medieval commune,* here independent urban republic (as in Italy and Germany), there taxable "third estate" of the monarchy (as in France), afterwards, in the period of manufacture proper, serving either the semi-feudal or the absolute monarchy as a counterpoise against nobility, and, in fact, cornerstone of the great monarchies in general, the bourgeoisie has at last, since the establishment of modern industry and of the world market, conquered for itself, in the modern representative state, exclusive political sway. The executive of the modern state is but a committee for managing the common affairs of the whole bourgeoisie.

The bourgeoisie, historically, has played a most revolutionary part.

The bourgeoisie, wherever it has got the upper hand, has put an end to all feudal, patriarchal, idyllic relations. It has pitilessly torn asunder the motley feudal ties that bound man to his "natural superiors," and has left no other nexus between man and man than naked self-interest, than callous "cash payment." It has drowned the most heavenly ecstasies of religious fervor, of chivalrous enthusiasm, of Philistine sentimentalism, in the icy water of egotistical calculation. It has resolved personal worth into exchange value, and in place of the numberless indefeasible chartered freedoms, has set up that single, unconscionable freedom—free trade. In one word, for exploitation, veiled by religious and political illusions, it has substituted naked, shameless, direct, brutal exploitation.

The bourgeoisie has stripped of its halo every occupation hitherto honored and looked up to with reverent awe. It has converted the physician, the lawyer, the priest, the poet, the man of science, into its paid wage laborers.

The bourgeoisie has torn away from the family its sentimental veil and has reduced the family relation to a mere money relation.

The bourgeoisie has disclosed how it came to pass that the brutal display of vigor in the Middle Ages, which reactionists so much admire, found its fitting complement in the most slothful indolence. It has been the first to show what man's activity can bring about. It has accomplished wonders far surpassing Egyptian pyramids, Roman aqueducts, and Gothic cathedrals; it has conducted expeditions that put in the shade all former exoduses of nations and crusades.

The bourgeoisie cannot exist without constantly revolutionizing the instruments of production, and thereby the relations of production, and with them the whole relations of society. Conservation of the old modes

---

*Commune was the name taken in France by the nascent towns even before they had conquered from their feudal lords and masters, local self-government and political rights as "the Third Estate." Generally speaking, for economical development of the bourgeoisie, England is here taken as the typical country, for its political development, France.

of production in unaltered form was, on the contrary, the first condition of existence for all earlier industrial classes. Constant revolutionizing of production, uninterrupted disturbance of all social conditions, everlasting uncertainty, and agitation distinguish the bourgeois epoch from all earlier ones. All fixed, fast frozen relations, with their train of ancient and venerable prejudices and opinions, are swept away, all new formed ones become antiquated before they can ossify. All that is solid melts into the air, all that is holy is profaned, and man is at last compelled to face with sober senses, his real conditions of life, and his relations with his kind.

The need of a constantly expanding market for its products chases the bourgeoisie over the whole surface of the globe. It must nestle everywhere, settle everywhere, establish connections everywhere.

The bourgeoisie has through its exploitation of the world market given a cosmopolitan character to production and consumption in every country. To the great chagrin of reactionists, it has drawn from under the feet of industry the national ground on which it stood. All old, established national industries have been destroyed or are daily being destroyed. They are dislodged by new industries, whose introduction becomes a life and death question for all civilized nations, by industries that no longer work up indigenous raw material, but raw material drawn from the remotest zones; industries whose products are consumed, not only at home, but in every quarter of the globe. In place of the old wants, satisfied by the productions of the country, we find new wants, requiring for their satisfaction the products of distant lands and climes. In place of the old local and national seclusion and self sufficiency, we have intercourse in every direction, universal interdependence of nations. And as in material, so also in intellectual production. The intellectual creations of individual nations become common property. National onesidedness and narrowmindedness become more and more impossible, and from the numerous national and local literatures, there arises a world literature.

The bourgeoisie by the rapid improvement of all instruments of production, by the immensely facilitated means of communication, draws all, even the most barbarian nations into civilization. The cheap prices of its commodities are the heavy artillery with which it batters down all Chinese walls, with which it forces the barbarians' intensely obstinate hatred of foreigners to capitulate. It compels all nations, on pain of extinction, to adopt the bourgeois mode of production; it compels them to introduce what it calls civilization into their midst, that is, to become bourgeois themselves. In a word, it creates a world after its own image.

The bourgeosie has subjected the country to the rule of the towns. It has created enormous cities, has greatly increased the urban population as compared with the rural and has thus rescued a considerable part of the population from the idiocy of rural life. Just as it has made the country dependent on the towns, so it has made barbarian and semi-barbarian countries dependent on civilized ones, nations of peasants on nations of bourgeois, the East on the West.

The bourgeoisie keeps more and more doing away with the scattered state of the population, of the means of production, and of property. It has agglomerated population, centralized means of production, and has concentrated property in a few hands. The necessary consequence of this was political centralization. Independent, or but loosely connected provinces, with separate interests, laws, governments, and systems of taxation, became lumped together in one nation, with one government, one code of laws, one national class interest, one frontier and one customs tariff.

The bourgeoisie, during its rule of scarce one hundred years, has created more massive and more colossal productive forces than have all preceding generations together. Subjection of nature's forces to man, machinery, application of chemistry to industry and agriculture, steam navigation, railways, electric telegraphs, clearing of whole continents for cultivation, canalization of rivers, whole populations conjured out of the ground—what earlier century had even a presentiment that such productive forces slumbered in the lap of social labor?

We see then: the means of production and of exchange on whose foundation the bourgeoisie built itself up, were generated in feudal society. At a certain stage in the development of these means of production and of exchange, the conditions under which feudal society produced and exchanged, the feudal organization of agriculture and manufacturing industry, in one word, the feudal relations of property became no longer compatible with the already developed productive forces; they became so many fetters. They had to burst asunder; they were burst asunder.

Into their places stepped free competition, accompanied by social and political constitution adapted to it, and by economical and political sway of the bourgeois class.

A similar movement is going on before our own eyes. Modern bourgeois society with its relations of production, of exchange and of property, a society that has conjured up such gigantic means of production and of exchange, is like the sorcerer, who is no longer able to control the powers of the nether world whom he has called up by his spells. For many a decade past, the history of industry and commerce is but the history of the revolt of modern productive forces against modern conditions of production, against the property relations that are the conditions for the existence of the bourgeoisie and of its rule. It is enough to mention the commercial crises that by their periodical return put on its trial, each time more threateningly, the existence of the entire bourgeois society. In these crises a great part, not only of the existing products, but also of the previously created productive forces, are periodically destroyed. In these crises there breaks out an epidemic that, in all earlier epochs, would have seemed an absurdity—the epidemic of overproduction. Society suddenly finds itself put back into a state of momentary barbarism; it appears as if a famine, a universal war of devastation, had cut off the supply of every means of subsistence; industry and commerce seem to be destroyed; and why? Because there is too much civilization, too much means of subsistence, too much industry, too much commerce. The productive forces at the disposal of society no longer tend to further the development of the conditions of the bourgeois property; on the contrary, they have become too powerful for these conditions by which they are fettered, and as soon as they overcome these fetters they bring disorder into the whole of bourgeois society, endanger the existence of bourgeois property. The conditions of bourgeois society are too narrow to comprise the wealth created by them. And how does the bourgeoisie get over these crises? On the one hand by enforced destruction of a mass of productive forces; on the other, by the conquest of new markets, and by the more thorough exploitation of the old ones. That is to say, by paving the way for more extensive and more destructive crises, and by diminishing the means whereby crises are prevented.

The weapons with which the bourgeoisie felled feudalism to the ground are now turned against the bourgeoisie itself.

But not only has the bourgeoisie forged the weapons that bring death to itself; it has also called into existence the men who are to wield those weapons--the modern working class--the proletarians.

In proportion as the bourgeoisie, that is, capital, is developed, in the same proportion is the proletariat, the modern working class, developed, a class of laborers who live only so long as they find work, and who find work only so long as their labor increases capital. These laborers, who must sell themselves piecemeal, are a commodity, like every other article of commerce, and are consequently exposed to all the vicissitudes of competition, to all the fluctuations of the market.

Owing to the extensive use of machinery and to division of labor, the work of the proletarians has lost all individual character, and consequently, all charm for the workman. He becomes an appendage of the machine, and it is only the most simple, most monotonous and most easily acquired knack that is required of him. Hence, the cost of production of a workman is restricted almost entirely to the means of subsistence that he requires for his maintenance, and for the propagation of his race. But the price of a commodity, and also of labor, is equal to its cost of production. In proportion, therefore, as the repulsiveness of the work increases the wage decreases. Nay more, in proportion as the use of machinery and division of labor increases, in the same proportion the burden of toil increases, whether by prolongation of the working hours, by increase of the work enacted in a given time, or by increased speed of the machinery, and so forth.

Modern industry has converted the little workshop of the patriarchal master into the great factory of the industrial capitalist. Masses of laborers, crowded into factories, are organized like soldiers. As privates of the industrial army they are placed under the command of a perfect hierarchy of officers and sergeants. Not only are they the slaves of the bourgeois class and of the bourgeois state, they are daily and hourly enslaved by the machine, by the overlooker, and above all, by the individual bourgeois manufacturer himself. The more openly this despotism proclaims gain to be its end and aim, the more petty, the more hateful and the more embittering it is.

The less the skill and exertion or strength implied in manual labor, in other words, the more modern industry becomes developed, the more is the labor of men superseded by that of women. Differences of age and sex have no longer any distinctive social validity for the working class. All are instruments of labor, more or less expensive to use, according to their age and sex.

No sooner is the exploitation of the laborer by the manufacturer, so far at an end, that he receives his wages in cash, than he is set upon by the other portions of the bourgeoisie, the landlord, the shopkeeper, the pawnbroker, and so forth.

The lower strata of the middle class—the small tradespeople, shopkeepers, and retired tradesmen generally, the handicraftsmen and peasants—all these sink gradually into the proletariat, partly because their diminutive capital does not suffice for the scale on which modern industry is carried on, and is swamped in the competition with the large capitalists, partly because their specialized skill is rendered worthless by new methods of production. Thus the proletariat is recruited from all classes of the population.

The proletariat goes through various stages of development. With its birth begins its struggle with the bourgeoisie. At first the contest is carried on by individual laborers, then by the workpeople of a factory, then by the operatives of one trade, in one locality, against the individual bourgeois who directly exploits them. They direct their attacks not against the bourgeois conditions of production, but against the instruments of production themselves; they destroy imported wares that compete with their labor, they smash to pieces machinery, they set factories ablaze, they seek to restore by force the vanished status of the workman of the Middle Ages.

At this stage the laborers still form an incoherent mass scattered over the whole country, and broken up by their mutual competition. If anywhere they unite to form more compact bodies, this is not yet the consequence of their own active union, but of the union of the bourgeoisie, which class, in order to attain its own political ends, is compelled to set the whole proletariat in motion, and is moreover yet, for a time, able to do so. At this stage, therefore, the proletarians do not fight their enemies, but the enemies of their enemies, the remnants of absolute monarchy, the landowners, the nonindustrial bourgeois, the petty bourgeoisie. Thus the whole historical movement is concentrated in the hands of the bourgeoisie; every victory so obtained is a victory for the bourgeoisie.

But with the development of industry the proletariat not only increases in number; it becomes concentrated in greater masses, its strength grows and it feels that strength more. The various interests and conditions of life within the ranks of the proletariat are more and more equalized, in proportion as machinery obliterates all distinctions of labor, and nearly everywhere reduces wages to the same low level. The growing competition among the bourgeois, and the resulting commercial crisis, make the wages of the workers even more fluctuating. The unceasing improvement of machinery, ever more rapidly developing, makes their livelihood more and more precarious; the collisions between individual workmen and individual bourgeois take more and more the character of collisions between two classes. Thereupon the workers begin to form combinations (Trades' Unions) against the bourgeois; they club together in order to keep up the rate of wages; they found permanent associations in order to make provision beforehand for these occasional revolts. Here and there the contest breaks out into riots.

Now and then the workers are victorious, but only for a time. The real fruit of their battle lies not in the immediate result but in the ever expanding union of workers. This union is helped on by the improved means of communication that are created by modern industry, and that places the workers of different localities in contact with one another. It was just this contact that was needed to centralize the numerous local struggles, all of the same character, into one national struggle between classes. But every class struggle is a political struggle. And that union, to attain which the burghers of the Middle Ages with their miserable highways, required centuries, the modern proletarians, thanks to railways, achieve in a few years.

This organization of the proletarians into a class, and consequently into a political party, is continually being upset again by the competition between the workers themselves. But it ever rises up again, stronger, firmer, mightier. It compels legislative recognition of particular interests of the workers by taking advantage of the divisions among the bourgeoisie itself. Thus the ten hours' bill in England was carried.

Altogether collisions between the classes of the old society further, in many ways, the course of development of the proletariat. The bourgeoisie finds itself involved in a constant battle. At first with the aristocracy; later on, with those portions of the bourgeoisie itself whose interests have become antagonistic to the progress of industry; at all times, with the bourgeoisie of foreign countries. In all these battles it sees itself compelled to appeal to the proletariat, to ask for its help, and thus, to drag it into the political arena. The bourgeoisie itself, therefore, supplies the proletariat with its own elements of political and general education; in other words, it furnishes the proletariat with weapons for fighting the bourgeoisie.

Further, as we have already seen, entire sections of the ruling classes are, by the advance of industry, precipitated into the proletariat, or are at least threatened in their conditions of existence. These also supply the proletariat with fresh elements of enlightenment and progress.

Finally, in times when the class struggle nears the decisive hour, the process of dissolution going on within the ruling class—in fact, within the whole range of an old society—assumes such a violent, glaring character that a small section of the ruling class cuts itself adrift and joins the revolutionary class, the class that holds the future in its hands. Just as, therefore, at an earlier period, a section of the nobility went over to the bourgeoisie, so now a portion of the bourgeoisie goes over to the proletariat, and in particular, a portion of the bourgeois ideologists, who have raised themselves to the level of comprehending theoretically the historical movements as a whole.

Of all the classes that stand face to face with the bourgeoisie today the proletariat alone is a really revolutionary class. The other classes decay and finally disappear in the face of modern industry; the proletariat is its special and essential product.

The lower middle class, the small manufacturer, the shopkeeper, the artisan, the peasant, all these fight against the bourgeoisie, to save from extinction their existence as fractions of the middle class. They are therefore not revolutionary, but conservative. Nay, more; they are reactionary, for they try to roll back the wheel of history. If by chance they are revolutionary, they are so only in view of their impending transfer into the proletariat; they thus defend not their present, but their future interests; they desert their own standpoint to place themselves at that of the proletariat.

The "dangerous class," the social scum, that passively rotting mass thrown off by the lowest layers of old society, may here and there, be swept into the movement by a proletarian revolution; its conditions of life, however, prepare it far more for the part of a bribed tool of reactionary intrigue.

In the conditions of the proletariat, those of the old society at large are already virtually swamped. The proletarian is without property; his relation to his wife and children has no longer anything in common with the bourgeois family relations; modern industrial labor, modern subjection to capital, the same in England as in France, in America as in Germany, has stripped him of every trace of national character. Law, morality, religion, are to him so many bourgeois prejudices, behind which lurk in ambush just as many bourgeois interests.

All the preceding classes that got the upper hand sought to fortify their already acquired status by subjecting society at large to their conditions of appropriation. The proletarians cannot become masters of the productive forces of society except by abolishing their own previous mode of appropriation, and thereby also every other previous mode of appropriation. They have nothing of their own to secure and to fortify; their mission is to destroy all previous securities for and insurances of individual property.

All previous historical movements were movements of minorities, or in the interest of minorities. The proletarian movement is the self-conscious, independent movement of the immense majority. The proletariat, the lowest stratum of our present society, cannot stir, cannot raise itself up without the whole superincumbent strata of official society being sprung into the air.

Though not in substance, yet in form, the struggle of the proletariat with the bourgeoisie is at first a national struggle. The proletariat of each country must, of course, first of all settle matters with its own bourgeoisie.

In depicting the most general phases of the development of the proletariat, we traced the more or less veiled civil war, raging within existing society, up to the point where that war breaks out into open revolution, and where the violent overthrow of the bourgeoisie lays the foundations for the sway of the proletariat.

Hitherto every form of society has been based, as we have already seen, on the antagonism of oppressing and oppressed classes. But in order to oppress a class, certain conditions must be assured to it under which it can, at least, continue its slavish existence. The serf, in the period of serfdom, raised himself to membership in the commune, just as the petty bourgeois, under the yoke of feudal absolutism managed to develop into a bourgeois. The modern laborer, on the contrary, instead of rising with the progress of industry, sinks deeper and deeper below the conditions of existence of his own class. He becomes a pauper, and pauperism develops more rapidly than population and wealth. And here it becomes evident that the bourgeoisie is unfit any longer to be the ruling class in society, and to impose its conditions of existence upon society as an overriding law. It is unfit to rule because it is incompetent to assure an existence to its slave within his slavery, because it cannot help letting him sink into such a state that it has to feed him, instead of being fed by him. Society can no longer live under this bourgeoisie; in other words, its existence is no longer compatible with society.

The essential condition for the existence and for the sway of the bourgeois class is the formation and augmentation of capital; the condition for capital is wage labor. Wage labor rests exclusively on competition between the laborers. The advance of industry, whose involuntary promoter is the bourgeoisie, replaces the isolation of the laborers, due to competition, by their involuntary combination, due to association. The development of modern industry, therefore, cuts from under its feet the very foundation on which the bourgeoisie produces and appropriates products. What the bourgeoisie therefore produces, above all, are its own grave diggers. Its fall and the victory of the proletariat are equally inevitable.

2 - PROLETARIANS AND COMMUNISTS

In what relation do the communists stand to the proletarians as a whole?

The communists do not form a separate party opposed to other working class parties.

They have no interests separate and apart from those of the proletariat as a whole.

They do not set up any sectarian principles of their own, by which to shape and mold the proletarian movement.

The communists are distinguished from the other working class par-

ties by this only:
1. In the national struggles of the proletarians of the different countries, they point out and bring to the front the common interests
   of the entire proletariat, independently of all nationality.
2. In the various stages of development which the struggle of the
   working class against the bourgeoisie has to pass through, they
   always and everywhere represent the interests of the movement as
   a whole.

The communists, therefore, are on the one hand practically the most
advanced and resolute section of the working class parties of every country, that section which pushes forward all others; on the other hand, theoretically, they have over the great mass of the proletariat the advantage
of clearly understanding the line of march, the conditions, and the ultimate general results of the proletarian movement.

The immediate aim of the communists is the same as that of all the
other proletarian parties: formation of the proletariat into a class, overthrow of the bourgeois of supremacy, conquest of political power by the
proletariat.

The theoretical conclusions of the communists are in no way based
on ideas or principles that have been invented or discovered by this or
that would-be universal reformer.

They merely express in general terms, actual relations springing from
an existing class struggle, from a historical movement going on under
our very eyes. The abolition of existing property relations is not at all a
distinctive feature of communism.

All property relations in the past have continually been subject to
historical change consequent upon the change in historical conditions.

The French Revolution, for example, abolished feudal property in favor of bourgeois property.

The distinguishing feature of communism is not the abolition of
property generally, but the abolition of bourgeois property. But modern
bourgeois private property is the final and most complete expression of
the system of producing and appropriating products, that is based on
class antagonism, on the exploitation of the many by the few.

In this sense, the theory of the communists may be summed up in the
single sentence: **Abolition of private property.**

We communists have been reproached with the desire of abolishing
the right of personally acquiring property as the fruit of a man's own labor, which property is alleged to be the groundwork of all personal freedom, activity, and independence.

Hard won, self acquired, self earned property! Do you mean the property of the petty artisan and of the small peasant, a form of property that preceded the bourgeois form? There is no need to abolish that; the development of industry has to a great extent already destroyed it and is still destroying it daily.

Or do you mean modern bourgeois private property?

But does wage labor create any property for the laborer? Not a bit. It creates capital, that is, that kind of property which exploits wage labor and which cannot increase except upon condition of getting a new supply of wage labor for fresh exploitation. Property, in its present form, is based on the antagonism of capital and wage labor. Let us examine both sides of this antagonism.

To be a capitalist is to have not only a purely personal, but a social status in production. Capital is a collective product, and only by the united action of many members, nay, in the last resort, only by the united action of all members of society, can it be set in motion.

Capital is therefore not a personal, it is a social power.

When, therefore, capital is converted into common property into the property of all members of society, personal property is not thereby transformed into social property. It is only the social character of the property that is changed. It loses its class character.

Let us now take wage labor.

The average price of wage labor is the minimum wage, that is, that quantum of the means of subsistence which is absolutely requisite to keep the laborer in bare existence as a laborer. What, therefore, the wage laborer appropriates by means of his labor, merely suffices to prolong and reproduce a bare existence. We by no means intend to abolish this personal appropriation of the products of labor, an appropriation that is made for the maintenance and reproduction of human life, and that leaves no surplus wherewith to command the labor of others. All that we want to do away with is the miserable character of this appropriation, under which the laborer lives merely to increase capital and is allowed to live only insofar as the interests of the ruling class require it.

In bourgeois society, living labor is but a means to increase accumulated labor. In communist society accumulated labor is but a means to widen, to enrich, to promote the existence of the laborer.

In bourgeois society, therefore, the past dominates the present; in communist society the present dominates the past. In bourgeois society, capital is independent and has individuality, while the living person is dependent and has no individuality.

And the abolition of this state of things is called by the bourgeois abolition of individuality and freedom! And rightly so. The abolition of bourgeois individuality, bourgeois independence, and bourgeois freedom is undoubtedly aimed at.

By freedom is meant, under the present bourgeois conditions of production, free trade, free selling and buying.

But if selling and buying disappears, free selling and buying disappears also. This talk about free selling and buying, and all the other "brave words" of our bourgeoisie about freedom in general have a meaning, if any, only in contrast with restricted selling and buying, with the fettered traders of the Middle Ages, but have no meaning when opposed to the communistic abolition of buying and selling, of the bourgeois conditions of production, and of the bourgeoisie itself.

You are horrified at our intending to do away with private property. But in your existing society private property is already done away with for nine-tenths of the population; its existence for the few is solely due to its nonexistence in the hands of those nine-tenths. You reproach us, therefore, with intending to do away with a form of property, the necessary condition for whose existence is the nonexistence of any property for the immense majority of society.

In one word, you reproach us with intending to do away with your property. Precisely so: That is just what we intend.

From the moment when labor can no longer be converted into capital, money, or rent, into a social power capable of being monopolized, that is, from the moment when individual property can no longer be transformed into bourgeois property, into capital, from that moment, you say, individuality vanishes.

You must, therefore, confess that by "individual" you mean no other person than the bourgeois, than the middle class owner of property. This person must, indeed, be swept out of the way and made impossible.

Communism deprives no man of the power to appropriate the products of society: all that it does is to deprive him of the power to subjugate the labor of others by means of such appropriation.

It has been objected that upon the abolition of private property all work will cease and universal laziness will overtake us.

According to this, bourgeois society ought long ago to have gone to the dogs through sheer idleness; for those of its members who work acquire nothing, and those who acquire anything do not work. The whole of this objection is but another expression of the tautology: that there can no longer be any wage labor when there is no longer any capital.

All objections urged against the communistic mode of producing and appropriating material products have, in the same way, been urged against the communistic modes of producing and appropriating intellectual products. Just as, to the bourgeois, the disappearance of class property is the disappearance of production itself, so the disappearance of class culture is to him identical with the disappearance of all culture.

That culture, the loss of which he laments, is, for the enormous majority, a mere training to act as a machine.

But don't wrangle with us so long as you apply, to our intended abolition of bourgeois property, the standard of your bourgeois notions of freedom, culture, law, and so forth. Your very ideas are but the outgrowth of the conditions of your bourgeois production and bourgeois property, just as your jurisprudence is but the will of your class made into a law for all, a will whose essential character and direction are determined by the economical conditions of existence of your class.

The selfish misconception that induces you to transform into eternal laws of nature and of reason the social forms springing from your present mode of production and form of property—historical relations that rise and disappear in the progress of production—that misconception you share with every ruling class that has preceded you. What you see clearly in the case of ancient property, what you admit in the case of feudal property, you are of course forbidden to admit in the case of your own bourgeois form of property.

Abolition of the family! Even the most radical flare up at this infamous proposal of the communists.

On what foundation is the present family, the bourgeois family, based? On capital, on private gain. In its completely developed form this family exists only among the bourgeoisie. But this state of things finds its complement in the practical absence of the family among the proletarians, and in public prostitution.

The bourgeois family will vanish as a matter of course when its complement vanishes, and both will vanish with the vanishing of capital.

Do you charge us with wanting to stop the exploitation of children by their parents? To this crime we plead guilty.

But, you will say, we destroy the most hallowed of relations when we replace home education by social.

And your education! Is not that also social, and determined by the social conditions under which you educate; by the intervention, direct or indirect, of society by means of schools, and so forth? The communists have not invented the intervention of society in education; they do but seek to alter the character of that intervention and to rescue education from the influence of the ruling class.

The bourgeois claptrap about the family and education, about the hallowed correlation of parent and child, become all the more disgusting, the more, by the action of modern industry, all family ties among the proletarians are torn asunder and their children transformed into simple articles of commerce and instruments of labor.

But you communists would introduce community of women [free love], screams the whole bourgeoisie chorus.

The bourgeois sees in his wife a mere instrument of production. He hears that the instruments of production are to be exploited in common, and, naturally, can come to no other conclusion, than that the lot of being common to all will likewise fall to the women.

He has not even a suspicion that the real point aimed at is to do away with the status of women as mere instruments of production.

For the rest, nothing is more ridiculous than the virtuous indignation of our bourgeois at the community of women, which, they pretend, is to be openly and officially established by the communists. The communists have no need to introduce community of women; it has existed almost from time immemorial.

Our bourgeois, not content with having the wives and daughters of their proletarians at their disposal, not to speak of common prostitutes, take the greatest pleasure in seducing each others' wives.

Bourgeois marriage is in reality a system of wives in common, and thus, at the most, what the communists might possibly be reproached with, is that they desire to introduce, in substitution for a hypocritically concealed, an openly legalized community of women. For the rest, it is self-evident that the abolition of the present system of production must bring with it the abolition of the community of women springing from that system, that is, of prostitution both public and private.

The communists are further reproached with desiring to abolish countries and nationalities.

The working men have no country. We cannot take from them what they don't possess. Since the proletariat must first of all acquire political supremacy, must rise to be the leading class of the nation, must constitute itself the nation, it is, so far, itself national, though not in the bourgeois sense of the word.

National differences and antagonisms between peoples are daily more and more vanishing, owing to the development of the bourgeoisie, to freedom of commerce, to the world market, to uniformity in the mode of production, and in the conditions of life corresponding thereto.

The supremacy of the proletariat will cause them to vanish still faster. United action, of the leading civilized countries at least, is one of the first conditions for the emancipation of the proletariat.

In proportion as the exploitation of one individual by another is put an end to, the exploitation of one nation by another will also be put an end to. In proportion as the antagonism between classes within the nation vanishes, the hostility of one nation to another will come to an end.

The charges against communism made from a religious, a philosophical, and generally, from an ideological standpoint, are not deserving of serious examination.

Does it require deep intuition to comprehend that man's ideas, views and conceptions, in one word, man's consciousness, changes with every change in the conditions of his material existence, in his social relations, and in his social life?

What else does the history of ideas prove than that intellectual production changes in character in proportion as material production is changed? The ruling ideas of each age have ever been the ideas of its ruling class.

When people speak of ideas that revolutionize society they do but express the fact that within the old society the elements of a new one have been created and that the dissolution of the old ideas keeps even pace with the dissolution of the old conditions of existence.

When the ancient world was in its last throes the ancient religions were overcome by Christianity. When Christian ideas succumbed in the eighteenth century to rationalist ideas, feudal society fought its death battle with the then revolutionary bourgeoisie. The ideas of religious liberty and freedom of conscience merely gave expression to the sway of free competition within the domain of knowledge.

"Undoubtedly," it will be said, "religious, moral, philosophical, and judicial ideas have been modified in the course of historical development. But religion, morality, philosophy, political science, and law constantly survived this change.

"There are, besides, eternal truths, such as freedom, justice and so forth, that are common to all states of society. But communism abolishes eternal truths, it abolishes all religion and all morality, instead of constituting them on a new basis; it therefore acts in contradiction to all past historical experience."

What does this accusation reduce itself to? The history of all past society has consisted in the development of class antagonisms, antagonisms that assumed different forms at different epochs.

But whatever form they may have taken, one fact is common to all past ages, namely, the exploitation of one part of society by the other. No wonder, then, that the social consciousness of past ages, despite all the multiplicity and variety it displays, moves within certain common forms, or general ideas, which cannot completely vanish except with the total disappearance of class antagonisms.

The communist revolution is the most radical rupture with traditional property relations; no wonder that its development involves the most radical rupture with traditional ideas.

But let us have done with the bourgeois objections to communism.

We have seen above that the first step in the revolution by the working class is to raise the proletariat to the position of ruling class, to win the battle of democracy.

The proletariat will use its political supremacy to wrest, by degrees, all capital from the bourgeoisie, to centralize all instruments of production in the hands of the state, that is, of the proletariat organized as a ruling class; and to increase the total productive forces as rapidly as possible.

Of course in the beginning, this cannot be effected except by means of despotic inroads on the rights of property and on the conditions of bourgeois production; by means of measures, therefore, which appear economically insufficient and untenable, but which in the course of the movement outstrip themselves, necessitate further inroads upon the old social order, and are unavoidable as a means of entirely revolutionizing the mode of production.

These measures will of course be different in different countries.

Nevertheless in the most advanced countries the following will be pretty generally applicable:

1. Abolition of property in land and application of all rents of land to public purposes.
2. A heavy progressive or graduated income tax.
3. Abolition of all right of inheritance.
4. Confiscation of the property of all emigrants and rebels.
5. Centralization of credit in the hands of the state, by means of a national bank with state capital and an exclusive monopoly.
6. Centralization of the means of communication and transport in the hands of the state.
7. Extension of factories and instruments of production owned by the state; the bringing into cultivation of waste lands, and the improvement of the soil generally in accordance with a common plan.
8. Equal liability of all to labor. Establishment of industrial armies, especially for agriculture.
9. Combination of agriculture with manufacturing industries; gradual

abolition of the distinction between town and country by a more
equable distribution of the population over the country.
10. Free education for all children in public schools. Abolition of
children's factory labor in its present form. Combination of education with industrial production, and so forth.

When in the course of development, class distinctions have disappeared, and all production has been concentrated in the hands of a vast
association of the whole nation, the public power will lose its political
character. Political power, properly so called, is merely the organized
power of one class for oppressing another. If the proletariat during its
contest with the bourgeoisie is compelled, by the force of circumstances
to organize itself as a class, if, by means of a revolution, it makes itself
the ruling class, and, as such, sweeps away by force the old conditions of
production, then it will, along with these conditions, have swept away
the conditions for the existence of class antagonism and of classes generally, and will thereby have abolished its own supremacy as a class.

In place of the old bourgeois society, with its classes and class antagonisms, we shall have an association in which the free development
of each is the condition for the free development of all.

3 - SOCIALIST AND COMMUNIST LITERATURE

1) reactionary socialism

(a) feudal socialism

Owing to their historical position, it became the vocation of the aristocracies of France and England to write pamphlets against modern bourgeois society. In the French revolution of July 1830, and in the English
reform agitation, these aristocracies again succumbed to the hateful up-
start. Thenceforth, a serious political contest was altogether out of the
question. A literary battle alone remained possible. But even in the
domain of literature the old cries of the restoration period* had become
impossible.

In order to arouse sympathy the aristocracy was obliged to lose sight,
apparently, of their own interests and to formulate their indictment
against the bourgeoisie in the interest of the exploited working class
alone. Thus the aristocrats took their revenge by singing lampoons on
their new master and whispering in his ears sinister prophecies of coming catastrophe.

In this way arose feudal socialism: half lamentation, half lampoon;
half echo of the past, half menace of the future; at times, by its bitter,

*Not the English Restoration, 1660 to 1689, but the French Revolution, 1814 to 1830.

witty and incisive criticism, striking the bourgeoisie to the very heart's core, but always ludicrous in its effect, through total incapacity to comprehend the march of modern history.

The aristocracy, in order to rally the people to them, waved the proletarian almsbag in front of a banner. But the people, so often as it joined them, saw on their hindquarters the old feudal coat of arms and deserted with loud and irreverent laughter.

One section of the French Legitimists, and "Young England," exhibited this spectacle.

In pointing out that their mode of exploitation was different to that of the bourgeoisie, the feudalists forget that they exploited under circumstances and conditions that were quite different and that are now antiquated. In showing that, under their rule, the modern proletariat never existed, they forget that the modern bourgeoisie is the necessary offspring of their own form of society.

For the rest, so little do they conceal the reactionary character of their criticism that their chief accusation against the bourgeoisie amounts to this, that under the bourgeois regime a class is being developed which is destined to cut up root and branch the old order of society.

What they upbraid the bourgeoisie with is not so much that it creates a proletariat as that it creates a revolutionary proletariat.

In political practice, therefore, they join in all coercive measures against the working class; and in ordinary life, despite their high falutin phrases, they stoop to pick up the golden apples dropped from the trees of industry and to barter truth, love, and honor for traffic in wool, beetroot sugar and potato spirit.*

As the parson has ever gone hand in hand with the landlord, so has clerical socialism with feudal socialism.

Nothing is easier than to give Christian asceticism a socialist tinge. Has not Christianity declaimed against private property, against marriage, against the state? Has it not preached, in the place of these, charity and poverty, celibacy and mortification of the flesh, monastic life and Mother Church? Christian socialism is but the holy water with which the priest consecrates the heartburnings of the aristocrat.

---

*This applies chiefly to Germany, where the landed aristocracy and squirearchy have large portions of their estates cultivated for their own account by stewards, and are, moreover, extensive beetroot sugar manufacturers and distillers of potato spirits. The wealthier British aristocracy are, as yet, rather above that; but they, too, know how to make up for declining rents by lending their names to floaters of more or less shady joint stock companies.

(b) petty bourgeois socialism

The feudal aristocracy was not the only class that was ruined by the bourgeoisie, not the only class whose conditions of existence pined and perished in the atmosphere of modern bourgeois society. The medieval burgesses and the small peasant bourgeoisie were the precursors of the modern bourgeoisie. In those countries which are but little developed, industrially and commercially, these two classes still vegetate side by side with the rising bourgeoisie.

In countries where modern civilization has become fully developed, a new class of petty bourgeoisie has been formed, fluctuating between proletariat and bourgeoisie, and ever renewing itself as a supplementary part of bourgeois society. The individual members of this class, however, are being constantly hurled down into the proletariat by the action of competition, and, as modern industry develops, they even see the moment approaching when they will completely disappear as an independent section of modern society, to be replaced, in manufactures, agriculture, and commerce, by overlookers, bailiffs, and shopmen.

In countries like France, where the peasants constitute far more than half of the population, it was natural that writers who sided with the proletariat against the bourgeoisie should use, in their criticism of the bourgeois regime, the standard of the peasant and petty bourgeois, and from the standpoint of these intermediate classes should take up the cudgels for the working class. Thus arose petty bourgeois socialism. Sismondi was the head of this school, not only in France, but also in England.

This school of socialism dissected with great acuteness the contradictions in the conditions of modern production. It laid bare the hypocritical apologies of economists. It proved incontrovertibly the disastrous effects of machinery and division of labor; the concentration of capital and land in a few hands; overproduction and crises; it pointed out the inevitable ruin of the petty bourgeois and peasant, the misery of the proletariat, the anarchy in production, the crying inequalities in the distribution of wealth, the industrial war of extermination between nations, the dissolution of old moral bonds, of the old family relations, of the old nationalities.

In its positive aims, however, this form of socialism aspires either to restoring the old means of production and of exchange, and with them the old property relations and the old society, or to cramping the modern means of production and of exchange, within the framework of the old property relations that have been, and were bound to be exploded by those means. In either case it is both reactionary and Utopian.

Its last words are: corporate guilds for manufacture; patriarchal relations in agriculture.

Ultimately, when stubborn historical facts had dispersed all intoxicating effects of self deception, this form of socialism ended in a miserable fit of the blues.

The socialist and communist literature of France, a literature that originated under the pressure of a bourgeoisie in power and that was the expression of the struggle against this power was introduced into Germany at a time when the bourgeoisie in that country had just begun its contest with feudal absolutism.

German philosophers, would-be philosophers, and *beaux esprits* eagerly seized on this literature, only forgetting that, when these writings emigrated from France into Germany, French social conditions had not emigrated along with them. In contact with German social conditions this French literature lost its immediate practical significance and assumed a purely literary aspect. Thus, to the German philosophers of the eighteenth century the demands of the first French revolution were nothing more than the demands of *practical reason* in general, and the utterance of the will of the revolutionary French bourgeoisie signified in their eyes the laws of pure will, of will as it was bound to be, of true human will generally.

The work of the German literati consisted solely in bringing the new French ideas into harmony with their ancient philosophical conscience, or, rather, in annexing the French ideas without deserting their own philosophic point of view.

This annexation took place in the same way in which a foreign language is appropriated, namely, by translation.

It is well known how the monks wrote silly lives of Catholic saints over the manuscripts on which the classical works of ancient heathendom had been written. The German literati reversed this process with the profane French literature. They wrote their philosophical nonsense beneath the French original. For instance, beneath the French criticism of the economic functions of money they wrote "Alienation of Humanity," and beneath the French criticism of the bourgeois state they wrote "Dethronement of the Category of the General," and so forth.

The introduction of these philosophical phrases at the back of the French historical criticisms they dubbed "philosophy of action," "true socialism," "German science of socialism," "philosophical foundation of socialism," and so on.

The French socialist and communist literature was thus completely emasculated. And, since it ceased in the hands of the German to express the struggle of one class with the other, he felt conscious of having

overcome "French one-sidedness" and of representing, not true requirements, but the requirements of truth, not the interests of the proletariat,
but the interests of human nature, of man in general, who belongs to no
class, has no reality, who exists only in the misty realm of philosophical fantasy.

This German socialism, which took its schoolboy task so seriously
and solemnly, and extolled its poor stock in trade in such mountebank
fashion, meanwhile gradually lost its pedantic innocence.

The fight of the German, and especially of the Prussian, bourgeoisie
against feudal aristocracy and absolute monarchy, in other words, the liberal movement, became more earnest.

By this, the long wished for opportunity was offered to "true socialism" of confronting the political movement with the socialist demands,
of hurling the traditional anathemas against liberalism, against representative government, against bourgeois competition, bourgeois freedom of
the press, bourgeois legislation, bourgeois liberty and equality, and of
preaching to the masses that they had nothing to gain and everything to
lose by this bourgeois movement. German Socialism forgot, in the nick
of time, that the French criticism, whose silly echo it was, presupposed
the existence of modern bourgeois society, with its corresponding economic conditions of existence, and the political constitution, adapted
thereto, the very things whose attainment was the object of the pending
struggle in Germany.

To the absolute governments, with their following of parsons, pro-
fessors, country squires, and officials, it served as a welcome scarecrow
against the threatening bourgeoisie.

It was a sweet finish after the bitter pills of floggings and bullets
with which these same governments, just at that time, dosed the German
working class risings.

While the "true" socialism thus served the governments as a weapon
for fighting the German bourgeoisie, it at the same time directly represented a reactionary interest, the interest of the German Philistines. In
Germany the petty bourgeois class, a relic of the sixteenth century, and
since then constantly cropping up again under various form, is the real
social basis of the existing state of things.

To preserve this class is to preserve the existing state of things in
Germany. The industrial and political supremacy of the bourgeoisie
threatens it with certain destruction; on the one hand, from the concentration of capital; on the other, from the rise of a revolutionary proletariat. "True" socialism appeared to kill these two birds with one stone. It
spread like an epidemic.

The robe of speculative cobwebs, embroidered with flowers of rhetoric, steeped in the dew of sickly sentiment, this transcendental robe in which the German socialists wrapped their sorry "eternal truths," all skin and bone, served to wonderfully increase the sale of their goods amongst such a public.

And on its part, German socialism recognized more and more its own calling as the bombastic representative of the petty bourgeois Philistine.

It proclaimed the German nation to be the model nation, and the German petty Philistine to be the typical man. To every villainous meanness of this model man it gave a hidden, higher, socialistic interpretation, the exact contrary of its true character. It went to the extreme length of directly opposing the "brutally destructive" tendency of communism, and of proclaiming its supreme and impartial contempt of all class struggle. With very few exceptions, all the so called socialist and communist publications that now (1847) circulate in Germany belong to the domain of this foul and enervating literature.

2) conservative or bourgeois socialism

A part of the bourgeoisie is desirous of redressing social grievances, in order to secure the continued existence of bourgeois society.

To this section belong economists, philanthropists, humanitarians, improvers of the condition of the working class, organizers of charity, members of societies for the prevention of cruelty to animals, temperance fanatics, hole and corner reformers of every imaginable kind. This form of socialism has, moreover, been worked out into complete systems.

We may cite Proudhon's *Philosophie de la Misere* as an example of this form.

The socialistic bourgeois want all the advantages of modern social conditions without the struggles and dangers necessarily resulting therefrom. They desire the existing state of society minus its revolutionary and disintegrating elements. They wish for a bourgeoisie without a proletariat. The bourgeoisie naturally conceives the world in which it is supreme to be the best; and bourgeois socialism develops this comfortable conception into various more or less complete systems. In requiring the proletariat to carry out such a system, and thereby to march straightway into the social New Jerusalem, it but requires in reality that the proletariat should remain within the bounds of existing society, but should cast away all its hateful ideas concerning the bourgeoisie.

A second and more practical, but less systematic, form of this socialism sought to depreciate every revolutionary movement in the eyes of the working class by showing that no mere political reform, but only a change in the material conditions of existence, in economical relations, could be of any advantage to them. By changes in the material conditions of existence this form of socialism, however, by no means signifies abolition of the bourgeois relations of production, an abolition that can be effected only by a revolution, but administrative reforms, based on the continued existence of these relations; reforms, therefore, that in no respect affect the relations between capital and labor, but, at the best, lessen the cost, and simplify the administrative work, of bourgeois government.

Bourgeois socialism attains adequate expression when, and only when, it becomes a mere figure of speech. Free trade: for the benefit of the working class. Protective duties: for the benefit of the working class. Prison reform: for the benefit of the working class. This is the last word and the only seriously meant word of bourgeois socialism.

It is summed up in the phrase: the bourgeois is a bourgeois—for the benefit of the working class.

3) critical-Utopian socialism and communism

We do not here refer to that literature which, in every great modern revolution, has always given voice to the demands of the proletariat: such as the writings of Babeuf and others.

The first direct attempts of the proletariat to attain its own ends, made in times of universal excitement, when feudal society was being overthrown, these attempts necessarily failed, owing to the then undeveloped state of the proletariat, as well as to the absence of the economic conditions for its emancipation, conditions that had yet to be produced, and could be produced by the impending bourgeois epoch alone. The revolutionary literature that accompanied these first movements of the proletariat had necessarily a reactionary character. It inculcated universal asceticism and social leveling in its crudest form.

The socialist and communist systems properly so called, those of St. Simon, Fourier, Owen, and others, spring into existence in the early undeveloped period, described above, of the struggle between proletariat and bourgeoisie (see Section I. Bourgeois and Proletarians).

The founders of these systems see indeed the class antagonisms, as well as the action of the decomposing elements in the prevailing form of society. But the proletariat, as yet in its infancy, offers to them the spectacle of a class without any historical initiative or any independent political movement.

Since the development of class antagonism keeps even pace with the development of industry, the economic situation, as they find it, does not as yet offer to them the material conditions for the emancipation of the proletariat. They therefore search after a new social science, after new social laws, that are to create these conditions.

Historical action is to yield to their personal inventive action, historically created conditions of emancipation to fantastic ones, and the gradual, spontaneous class organization of the proletariat to an organization of society specially contrived by these inventors. Future history resolves itself, in their eyes, into the propaganda and the practical carrying out of their social plans.

In the formation of their plans they are conscious of caring chiefly for the interests of the working class, as being the most suffering class. Only from the point of view of being the most suffering class does the proletariat exist for them.

The undeveloped state of the class struggle, as well as their own surroundings, cause socialists of this kind to consider themselves far superior to all class antagonisms. They want to improve the condition of every member of society, even that of the most favored. Hence, they habitually appeal to society at large, without distinction of class; nay, by preference, to the ruling class. For how can people, when once they understand their system, fail to see in it the best possible plan of the best possible state of society?

Hence, they reject all political, and especially all revolutionary action; they wish to attain their ends by peaceful means, and endeavor, by small experiments, necessarily doomed to failure, and by the force of example to pave the way for the new social gospel.

Such fantastic pictures of future society, painted at a time when the proletariat is still in a very undeveloped state and has but a fantastic conception of its own position, correspond with the first instinctive yearnings of that class for a general reconstruction of society.

But these socialist and communist publications contain also a critical element. They attack every principle of existing society. Hence they are full of the most valuable materials for the enlightenment of the working class. The practical measures proposed in them, such as the abolition of the distinction between town and country, of the family, of the carrying on of industries for the account of private individuals, and of the wage system, the proclamation of social harmony, the conversion of the functions of the state into a mere superintendence of production, all these proposals point solely to the disappearance of class antagonisms which were at that time only just cropping up, and which, in these publications, are recognized under the earliest, indistinct, and undefined forms only. These proposals, therefore, are of a purely Utopian character.

The significance of critical-Utopian socialism and communism bears

an inverse relation to historical development. In proportion as the modern class struggle develops and takes definite shape, this fantastic standing apart from the contest, these fantastic attacks on it lose all practical
value and all theoretical justification. Therefore, although the originators
of these systems were in many respects revolutionary, their disciples
have in every case formed mere reactionary sects. They hold fast by the
original views of their masters, in opposition to the progressive historical development of the proletariat. They, therefore, endeavor, and that
consistently, to deaden the class struggle and to reconcile the class antagonisms. They still dream of experimental realization of their social
Utopias, of founding isolated "Phalansteres," of establishing "home colonies," of setting up a "Little Icaria"*—duodecimo editions of the New Jerusalem, and to realize all these castles in the air they are compelled to
appeal to the feelings and purses of the bourgeois. By degree they sank
into the category of the reactionary conservative socialists depicted
above, differing from these only by more systematic pedantry, and by
their fanatical and superstitious belief in the miraculous effects of their
social science.

The communists, therefore, violently oppose all political action on the part of
the working class; such action, according to them, can only result from
blind unbelief in the new gospel.

The Owenites in England and the Fourierists in France, respectively
oppose the Chartists and the "Reformistes."

4 - POSITION OF THE COMMUNISTS IN RELATION TO
THE VARIOUS EXISTING OPPOSITION PARTIES

Section 2 has made clear the relations of the communists to the existing working class parties, such as the Chartists in England and the agrarian reforms in America.

The communists fight for the attainment of the immediate aims, for
the enforcement of the momentary interests of the working class; but in
the movement of the present they also represent and take care of the future of that movement. In France the communists ally themselves with
the social democrats** against the conservative and radical bourgeoisie,

*Phalansteres were socialist colonies on the plan of Charles Fourier. Icaria
was the name given by Cabet to his Utopia and, later on, to his American
Communist colony.
**The party then represented in parliament by Ledru-Rollin, in literature by
Louis Blanc, in the daily press by the Reforme. The name of Social Democracy
signified, with these its inventors, a section of the Democratic or Republican
party more or less tinged with Socialism.

reserving, however, the right to take up a critical position in regard to phrases and illusions traditionally handed down from the great Revolution.

In Switzerland they support the radicals, without losing sight of the fact that this party consists of antagonistic elements, partly of democratic socialists, in the French sense, partly of radical bourgeois.

In Poland they support the party that insists on an agrarian revolution, as the prime condition for national emancipation, that party which fomented the insurrection of Cracow in 1846.

In Germany they fight with the bourgeoisie whenever it acts in a revolutionary way, against the absolute monarchy, the feudal squirearchy, and the petty bourgeoisie.

But they never cease for a single instant to instill into the working class the clearest possible recognition of the hostile antagonism between bourgeoisie and proletariat, in order that the German workers may straightway use, as so many weapons against the bourgeoisie, the social and political conditions that the bourgeoisie must necessarily introduce along with its supremacy, and in order that, after the fall of the reactionary classes in Germany, the fight against the bourgeoisie itself may immediately begin.

The communists turn their attention chiefly to Germany, because that country is on the eve of a bourgeois revolution, that is bound to be carried out under more advanced conditions of European civilization, and with a more developed proletariat, than that of England was in the seventeenth and of France in the eighteenth century, and because the bourgeois revolution in Germany will be but the prelude to an immediately following proletarian revolution.

In short, the communists everywhere support every revolutionary movement against the existing social and political order of things.

In all these movements they bring to the front, as the leading question in each, the property question, no matter what its degree of development at the time.

Finally, they labor everywhere for the union and agreement of the democratic parties of all countries.

The communists disdain to conceal their views and aims. They openly declare that their ends can be attained only by the forcible overthrow of all existing social conditions. Let the ruling classes tremble at a communistic revolution. The proletarians have nothing to lose but their chains. They have a world to win.

Working men of all countries, unite!

Edgar Bauer uses poetic license to describe Marx:

POWER SALUTE

Who comes rushing in, impetuous and wild—
Dark fellow from Trier, in fury raging,
Nor walks nor skips, but leaps upon his prey
In tearing rage, as one who leaps to grasp
Broad spaces of the sky and drag them down to earth,
Stretching his arms wide open to the heavens.
His evil fist is clenched, he roars interminably
As though ten thousand devils had him by the hair.

The poet was a fellow member of "the Doctors' Club,"
a group of Young Hegelians at the University of Berlin

from "Who comes rushing in," *Karl Marx in Berlin*, p. 75
Marx, Robert Payne

Marx hates bourgeois capitalists:
"I still remember the cutting, scornful tone with which
he uttered—I might almost say 'spat' the word bourgeois.
And he denounced as bourgeois—that is to say, as an un-
mistakable example of the lowest moral and spiritual stag-
nation—everyone who dared to oppose his opinions."
—young American, Carl Schurz
later a senator

his targeted enemies

MARX HATES CAPITALISM AND THE BOURGEOIS

Marx defines capitalism

Marx scorned capitalism and the bourgeois, who promoted it. He devoted most of his life's work to writing critically about this economic system in his book *Capital.*

In the early Industrial Revolution, Marx saw capitalism at its worst. He was born into a new era when water and steam power had changed the way people lived. Machines replaced the handicraft system. Vast cities grew up overnight. With poor social conditions accompanying rapid growth, Marx became pessimistic about capitalism's future. England, where change first began, suffered most. Children worked long hours in noisy, dirty, poorly ventilated factories; women worked for low wages; and heads of households faced a brand new threat, unemployment.

Though conditions of that time would shock today's citizen; nevertheless, compared to rural and village life at that time, life in the cities did not look so bad, according to Anatole Mazour and others. And though after this unsettled transition era, workers benefited from the industrial revolution, Marx did not live to see the full extent of improvement. He did not have the perspective of that period that modern historians and economists enjoy.

Marx's defining of capitalism, therefore, differs from that of modern scholars. Present day authors, Robert Lekachman and Borin Van Loon in *Capitalism for Beginners,* define capitalism with these three elements:

(1) Capital is wealth that is manmade and therefore reproducible.
(2) The means of production is privately owned.
(3) It works in a market system to establish income levels, wages, rents, profits
(For more about the market system, see chart 7, page 72.)

Marx, on the other hand, defines capitalism primarily in terms of class struggle. He sees capitalism as an economic system ruling over class conflict between the bourgeoisie and the proletariat. *By his definition, capitalism could not exist before the 1500s* because a single, definite, exploited, and opposing proletariat class did not arise until that time. "The historical conditions of capitalism's existence are by no means given with the mere circulation of money and commodities," he writes. "It can spring into life only when the owner of the means of production and subsistence meets in the market with the free laborer selling his labor power." The capitalist mode of production depends on a large labor force free to be employed because it has nothing to sell but its own labor; the propertyless proletariat is as necessary to capitalism as is accumulated capital for the ruling class, Marx explains.

Modern theoreticians, on the other hand, look at capitalism as a universal, ancient, and ongoing system, not as a recent, passing phase. They say that early man met the requisites for capitalism when he produced more than enough for his own household and looked for trade on the open market. This happened at the dawn of time, says Jean-Francois Revel in *How Democracies Perish.* Capitalism, he says, grew out of tradition, which modified and brought together "myriad individual fragments" for modern man to assemble finally into a general concept. "Capitalism is a bundle of modes of economic behavior," Revel writes. In contrast he calls communism a unified ideological system clamped violently on societies that do not want it.

Marxist scholar Robert Heilbroner says modern capitalism differs from earlier forms because of its pervasiveness of the total society. "For the market system is not just a means of exchanging goods; it is a mechanism for sustaining and maintaining an entire society," he writes. He gives a fascinating account of the development of capitalism in his book, *The Worldly Philosophies.* Nevertheless, ancient and modern capitalism, though differing in developmental level, share this common ground: private ownership of property and the flourishing of commerce.

Mazour and Peoples in *Men and Nations,* a world history, reflect the modern view in defining capitalism and tracing its origin: "Capital is wealth earned, saved, and invested in order to produce profits."

CHART 7: A BOURGEOIS VIEW OF HOW THE MARKET WORKS

With change being the norm in this information age, corporations have to be flexible to survive. Warren Buffett of Berkshire Hathaway holding company is an innovator with a reputation for wit as well as wisdom. In his annual report, he explains free enterprise with a character named Mr. Market .

"Ben Graham, my friend and teacher, long ago described the mental attitude toward market fluctuations that I believe to be most conducive to investment success. He said that you should imagine market quotations as coming from a remarkably accommodating fellow named Mr. Market who is your partner in a private business. Without fail, Mr. Market appears daily and names a price at which he will either buy your interest or sell you his.

"Even though the business that the two of you own may have economic characteristics that are stable, Mr. Market's quotations will be anything but. For, sad to say, the poor fellow has incurable emotional problems. At times he feels euphoric and can see only the favorable factors affecting the business. When in that mood, he names a very high buy-sell price because he fears that you will snap up his interest and rob him of imminent gains. At other times he is depressed and can see nothing but trouble ahead for both the business and the world. On these occasions he will name a very low price, since he is terrified that you will unload your interest on him.

"Mr. Market has another endearing characteristic: He doesn't mind being ignored. If his quotation is uninteresting to you today, he will be back with a new one tomorrow. Transactions are strictly at your option. Under these conditions, the more manic-depressive his behavior, the better for you.

"But, like Cinderella at the ball, you must heed one warning or everything will turn into pumpkins and mice: Mr. Market is there to serve you, not to guide you. It is his pocketbook, not his wisdom, that you will find useful. If he shows up some day in a particularly foolish mood, you are free to either ignore him or to take advantage of him, but it will be disastrous if you fall under his influence. Indeed, if you aren't certain that you understand and can value your business far better than Mr. Market, you don't belong in the game. As they say in poker, 'If you've been in the game thirty minutes and you don't know who the patsy is, *you're* the patsy.'"

Looking for good relationships as well as sound financial policy,* Mr. Buffett and co-chairman of the board, Charles Munger, illustrate by example the increased attention given by companies today to their philosophy base. In emphasizing the human factor in selling off businesses, Mr. Buffett says that he and Mr. Munger view investment in successful controlled businesses to be a permanent part of Berkshire rather than merchandise to be disposed of once Mr. Market offers a sufficiently high price." The co-chairmen give similar consideration to the leadership of their companies.

"Our attitude," he writes, "fits our personalities and the way we want to live our lives. Churchill once said, 'You shape your houses and then they shape you.' We know the manner in which we wish to be shaped. For that reason, we would rather achieve a return of X while associating with people whom we strongly like and admire than realize 110% of X by exchanging these relationships for uninteresting or unpleasant ones."

*The thesis of *In Pursuit of Excellence* is that successful companies do not traffic in "human" merchandise but value human relationships.

Quoted portions © 1988 by Warren E. Buffett. Reproduced, with permission, from the 1987 Annual Report to Stockholders of Berkshire Hathaway Inc.

"Capitalism is the economic system in which private individuals use wealth in this way. Capitalism did not suddenly appear during the Middle Ages. It dates back to man's earliest business activities, and certainly existed during Greek and Roman times. But it became more important in the later Middle Ages than it had been before," they write.

capitalism in history

To establish the timeframe of the far-flung, ancient capitalist Roman Empire, let's look at the midpoint of its approximate thousand year rule. That year coincides with the birth of Jesus into Israel, a subject nation of the empire. That midpoint year also marks the beginning of two hundred years of peace.

These early Romans created conditions favorable to the growth of capitalism. With the building of roads and bridges and the issuing of a universal passport, foreign trade and foreign travel increased. Eventually, giant businesses in agriculture, banking, trade, and manufacturing developed. With the establishment in member nations of limited voting rights, a postal service, a uniform code for law and order, and a common coinage, the republic stabilized. And this stability contributed to continued capitalist growth.

The Roman rule by law with limited government and a measure of freedom created the above conditions favorable to the development of commercial capitalism. Conversely, with the breakdown of this infrastructure, Roman society disappeared. Disintegration of the thousand year Roman Empire led to the ceasing of all but local trade.

England, for one, in the ensuing thousand year period of feudalism, divided up into small territories presided over by manors where nobles banded under feudal lords for mutual support and protection against constantly warring factions; serfs became bound to the land; that is, if the land changed ownership, the serfs remained and served new masters.

Not until the 1500s did feudalistic serfdom end and commerce completely revive. At that time the arts, science, and manufacturing of civilization again moved forward. Marx points to this time as the beginning of capitalism.

"new economic policies" in Marxism

Because Marx resisted that most important revolution, the Industrial

Revolution, Walter Lippmann calls him a counterrevolutionary. Marx resisted because he never grasped the inner principles of capitalism. By changing names on title deeds of private property, Marx thought he could right social wrongs. He thought he could steal the reins of capitalism and retain the wealth. But an economy, like some animals removed from their natural habitat, will not reproduce in captivity.

Jean-Francois Revel *(How Democracies Perish)* uses a stronger analogy than captivity. "Communism," he writes, "is not an economic system; it is a political system that must necessarily asphyxiate an economy." Carrying his analogy further, you might say that after you kill the economy, it doesn't matter whose name is on the title deed of the animal or what method you use to milk it. It won't produce.

Marx failed to see that without division of labor into specialized tasks, working through the market, a modern economy cannot function. Because he didn't understand economics he had no workable plan beyond revolution. All he could do, says Lippmann, was attack capitalism and impair the economy. Beyond that, collectivism doesn't work except under two extreme conditions: war or famine. The reason it works under those conditions is that extreme hardship mobilizes people and thus automatically regulates the economy. But in normal times, Lippmann says communists "must return to the division of labor in an exchange economy as surely as the farmer must return to his land if he would harvest a crop."

Lippmann's decades-old axiom has proved itself. Because Lenin had no guidance from Marx beyond revolution, he had to improvise his plans as he went along and soon had to revert to "new economic policies (NEP)," a euphemistic phrase for capitalist policies. And all communist leaders since, including Deng Xiaoping and Mikhail Gorbachev today, have had to resort to market practices and aid from capitalist countries to bail out their economies.

capitalism, Marxism, and exploitation

What Marx deplored was "bourgeois exploitation." "The laborer himself," Marx writes, "creates the fund out of which the capitalist pays him." Marx measures a capitalist's wealth by the amount of surplus labor expended to produce it and places capitalist wealth in direct ratio

to the measure of labor "exploitation." Here Marx reveals no understanding of a basic principle of capitalism—that not all value resides in
labor.

Ayn Rand *(Capitalism: the unknown ideal)* recognized this principle. She claims society's wealth depends upon entrepreneurs, who, by
seeking their own good, benefit others. Her writings condemn
confiscating wealth from these creators of it.

Economist Thomas Sowell *(Marxism)*, also, confronts Marxist
theory. If accumulated labor output measures wealth, then countries
with more labor hours and more diligent laborers would have a better
economy and a higher standard of living, or wealth, than countries with
less labor-intensive economies. But that is not the case, Sowell says.
The opposite is true. Some Third World countries, even with large
labor pools and capital transfers from advanced nations, have not been
able to create wealth or expand their capital. On the other hand, Japan
and some countries in the West, without physical capital, have created
wealth with mental capital. Managerial/investment/marketing skills and
work-ethic heritage make the difference. Marx ignores these factors.

capitalism:
incentive, accountability, voluntary association, mutual benefit

Marx leaves another essential element out of his equation for the
best economy. He doesn't take into account incentive to produce. He
fails to see that capitalism offers strong motivation to create wealth and
that communism stifles that impulse.

What makes the difference in go-power? Detractors say greed is the
motor that makes capitalism roll, but economist George Gilder says
that unless an entrepreneur is willing to give without guarantee of
return he cannot create wealth. "Confusing the creation and investing of
wealth with the seizing and hoarding of it is the problem of many
viewing capitalism," Gilder says.

Nevertheless, whether for noble designs or not, self-interest sparks
capitalism. But hand in hand with the privilege of self-interest goes the
duty of personal responsibility for all parties. In the merciless marketplace, where political agendas and collective decisions do not shield
power wielders, participants find no place to hide from accountability.

Unlike government controlled activity, marketplace business must meet the requirements of the bottom line or cease to exist.

Besides providing incentive and demanding accountability, capitalism offers a third important advantage, voluntary association. In the free market, parties exchange without coercion. And, "provided the transaction is bilaterally voluntary and informed," says economist Milton Friedman, both parties benefit.

Incentive to produce wealth is essential to a healthy economy. Accountability to the impartial, impersonal arbiter, the market, stabilizes the economy. Voluntary association requires excellence to attract buyers. And the prospect of mutual benefit attracts involvement and produces wealth.

Will capitalism live or die?

Although Marx's defining of *capitalism* has not endured, except among his followers, the perjorative connotation he has given the term lives on. The shadow lingers because Marx defined capitalism before its proponents did. Though Adam Smith in the 1700s wrote with uncanny foresight about free enterprise, for many years capitalism has existed without adequate philosophic and moral underpinnings. "Capitalism is being destroyed because it does not identify itself," says Ayn Rand.

About this strategy of Marx and his followers to discredit capitalism, Jean-Francois Revel makes this observation: "If all that need be done to legitimize communism is to show that capitalism has its faults, its vices and crises, then let's turn world power over to the communists at once on the principle that the best way to correct a limp is to cut off both legs."

Marx made his negative assessment of capitalism because he did not foresee the flexibility of modern capitalism; he based his theory on a rigid model. He didn't know what we know, that capitalism adapts to current conditions. Nor did he know how capitalism, an economic system, and democracy, a political system, work together to bend with the times. They work well together because they share a common base of rule by law, limited government control, and a measure of personal freedoms. Capitalism, in fact, tends toward democracy; Taiwan is an example. Students demonstrating in China for democracy is another.

Today many countries recognize the advantages of the free market. African, Asian, and Latin American countries turn to free market practices to improve their economies. But will that always be true? Marx predicted the capitalist system would eventually self-destruct because his bourgeois enemies would dig their own graves.

Is this likely to happen? No, answers George Gilder. "Capitalism, like the family, is not an institution that can become obsolete or decrepit as long as human societies persist," he writes. The Bible, in its last book seems to back his statement. *Merchants* at the end of time mourn the destruction of Babylon because "no one buys their merchandise anymore."

Since capitalism began in man's earliest social contacts and has continued ever since, it has proved its staying power as a system. Nonetheless, individual capitalist democracies will write their own death sentence if they fall down on key points. They'll self-destruct if they refuse to face the facts of history and ignore the goal of Marxist global expansion. Moreover, they'll fail if they throw commonsense out the window and consistently appease communist demands to their own harm. And what nation can survive if its populace lose a moral consensus and respect for authority, hard work, thrift, and independence? Such nations will fulfill Marx's prediction of capitalist suicide. "They sow the wind and reap the whirlwind."

But Marx is only partly right in his pessimistic predictions about the collapse of the capitalist system. Though the system may endure, individual nations will choose to be deceived. And the lies they believe will spell their doom.

his influence

MARX

a system new to mankind

Marx's ideas first took root in Russia. "October 25, 1917, must be marked as a redletter day," writes Mikhail Heller in *Cogs in the Wheel*. "On that day, for the first time in history, a revolution was carried out whose goal was not simply to seize power over what Lenin called the 'state machine,' *but to create an ideal society,* a political, economic and social system new to mankind." From that Soviet beachhead, Marxism has rippled out. It now claims fifty-plus nations.*

Marxism, a total, closed, politicized system, encompasses every department of life. "In our society whatever serves the interests of communism is moral," said Soviet Brezhnev, a Marxist, who fused politics and morals. Mikhail Gorbachev says it this way: "Our party must have a strong social policy embracing every aspect of a man's life."

global influence and expansion

Empires used to grow to a point of equilibrium, says Jean-Francois Revel, but not any more. For Marxists that point will not come until they dominate the world. Meanwhile, to mobilize the population and stimulate the economy, they maintain a common outside enemy threat. At one time Soviets claimed China was the threat; at another time, Germany; then, America; since World War II, the Jews. Recently, the USSR in the United Nations called Zionism a form of racism. So reports Mikhail Heller. With citizens steeped in fear, "hatred is cultivated as an essential, obligatory quality in a Soviet person," Heller says.

Toward their goal of world domination—according to the U.S. State Department**—Soviets engage in worldwide *active measures* through front organizations, friendship societies, disinformation, forgeries, education programs, churches, peace movements, and other organizations. Active measures support Soviet policy but are distinct from espionage,

*See Chart 8, page 79 for listing of nations and dates.   **See bibliography.

counterintelligence, and diplomacy.

Marxist front organizations hide behind ethnic titles and labels like peace, justice, social responsibility. Their hidden agenda is to recruit and influence noncommunists to carry out party agenda. Front groups serve two purposes, theoretician Hannah Arendt says: first, to manipulate noncommunists without revealing to them the true aims of the group and second, with this support from outsiders, to give communist members an illusion of normalcy about their radical behavior. The State Department says the success of Soviet active measures guarantees their future.

A highly successful active measure is the worldwide *peace movement.* Although Soviets do not allow peace demonstrations at home except with foreign delegations, they support the movement abroad. Such activism began with the first USSR leader, Lenin, and succeeds because targeted opponents cannot prove the hidden Marxist link. Because demonstrations imply the host government opposes peace, they create division, then gain sympathy for Marxist aims. Thus Soviets disarm their enemies; they convince their following that the USSR wants peace and is dangerous only when it believes it is being attacked. With this line, Marxists can expand their influence without resistance.

influence in America

Exiled Aleksander Solzhenitzyn explains what makes a country succumb to Marxist delusion. He says once society denies God and makes man supreme, it loses its moorings. Destabilization opens the way for moral and societal disintegration. Relativism is the step in this direction. "There is one thing a professor can be absolutely certain of," says Professor Allan Bloom in *The Closing of the American Mind:* "Almost every student entering the university believes. . . that truth is relative. . . . The danger they have been taught to fear from absolutism is not error but intolerance. . . The true believer is the real danger. . . The point is not to correct the mistakes and really be right; rather it is not to think you are right at all."

With the confusion relativism brings, says Ignace Lepp *(From Marxism to Christianity),* many become skeptics. Then, having lost the guiding hand of faith, the choice becomes the path of least resis-

CHART 8: COMMUNIST EXPANSION—countries/years

Invasion or revolution under Marx's banner—according to the 1983 Soviet publication, *Soviet Statistical Handbook*—has claimed these fifty-eight countries:

On October 25, 1917, Russia.

From 1920-1924 ten more absorbed into the Soviet Union. And one other, Mongolia, separate from the Soviet Union.

In 1940 four more part of the Soviet Union.

In 1946-1948 Eastern bloc countries: Albania, Bulgaria, Yugoslavia, Poland, Romania, Czechoslovakia, North Korea.

In 1949, China, East Germany, and Hungary. In 1951, Tibet absorbed by China.

In 1954-1958 North Vietnam, Guinea.
In 1960s: Cuba, Algeria, Burma, Tanzania, Congo, Mali, Syria, Libya, South Yemen.

In 1970s: Guyana, Iraq, Afghanistan*, Zambia, Ethiopia, Angola, Cambodia, Guinea-Bissau, Laos, Madagascar, Mozambique, Sao Tome/Principe, South Vietnam, Benin, Seychelles, Nicaragua.

In 1980-1983: Cape Verde, Zimbabwe, Ghana, Burkina Faso.

Comparatively, these eight have more freedom than the others: Poland, Hungary, Guyana, Zambia, Madagascar, Nicaragua, Cape Verde, and Zimbabwe.

*Since 1983, there have been unprecedented withdrawals in some places such as Afghanistan but continued revolution in many places not listed, such as in the Phillipines, El Salvador.

tance. Patrick Henry's dictum—"Give me liberty or give me death"—today gives way to *I'm comfortable with this* or *I'm not comfortable with that*. The goal is to adjust. This absence of faith and morality leaves a vacuum, which nature cannot tolerate. Therefore, many look to Marxism for a unifying principle of their existence, Lepp says.

On the subject of moral disorientation, Paul Johnson in *Modern Times* says, "Marx, Freud, Einstein all conveyed the same message to the 1920s: The world was not what it seemed. The senses, whose empirical perceptions shaped our ideas of time and distance, right and wrong, law and justice, and the nature of man's behavior in society, were not to be trusted. . . The exercise of individual free will ceases to be the supremely interesting feature of human behavior." And freedom loses its appeal. Wishful thinking then replaces reason, begets arguments against free enterprise, and attracts followers to Marx.

Why bring up the subject when Mikhail Gorbachev is promoting *glasnost* and *perestroika*? And when communist forces are pulling back in many parts of the world? Jean-Francois Revel pinpoints the problem. He says that whereas America concentrates intermittently and changeably, "communism scores its points because it thinks of nothing else." Democracy, he says—though on the defensive against an all-out totalitarian offensive—dares not admit it is fighting. It refuses to name totalitarianism for the menace it is, Revel warns.

influence in Hong Kong

Hong Kong, the epitome of the capitalist system, will soon fall under communist control. On the eve of the 1997 title transfer of Hong Kong from the jurisdiction of England to that of China, citizens there express fear about the future. Not all Americans, however, understand why those in Hong Kong feel as they do. At a 1988 conference this writer attended in San Francisco, the American discussant professor chastised a panel of leading figures from Hong Kong. "You panelists forecast the future of Hong Kong in pessimistic tones. None of us are seers. We don't know what's going to happen in the future. I challenge you to tell me: 'Where is the evidence that these terrible things are going to come to pass?'" He paused. "Where is the evidence? Show me!"

In the audience, an educator next to me from a university in Hong

Kong jumped to her feet and in a British accent threw the question back at the challenger. "And where is the evidence that these things will not come to pass?" she demanded.

This was an Asian studies convention, a group that sorts through details from thousands of years ago. Everyone knows the rules: Each audience participant states his identity and who he represents before speaking. But my seatmate with a point to get across had dismissed proprieties; and nobody stopped her. Others then spoke their mind.

After heated exchange, one panelist stepped to the microphone. He currently served on a legislative council to work out differences between Hong Kong and China in drawing up the Basic Law. Because China was trying to sidestep its pledge to the United Kingdom concerning Hong Kong's Basic Law, he and others in Hong Kong were pushing China to keep its promises. With strong words still hanging in the air, this gentleman tarried. The audience quieted down. Everyone waited.

In response to the question asking for evidence pointing to a dark future for Hong Kong, the panelist spoke in a low controlled tone of voice, "By the time there is some evidence. . ." He paused and looked around at the audience. Tension mounted before he finished. "I will already be in jail," he said.

That word climaxed the day. A clapping audience honored this man who knew whereof he spoke. Like many others in Hong Kong, his family had earlier fled from the mainland to freedom.

influence in Marxist lands

Under communism, instead of supply and demand governing the marketplace, Marxian government owns and controls every part of the economy. With *central planning,* usually in Five Year Plans, government dictates to factories, farms, and towns what to produce, for whom, how much, wages, and prices. (To fix prices, however, Marxists depend on free economies for price information that only the market yields.)

Local conditions vary according to resources, population distribution, and other factors. But all the citizenry are wage earning laborers whether professionals or workers. All these, according to time spent, earn workpoints to gain access to their work unit's storehouses. What is available to them depends upon the work unit to which they are assigned. (At times, however, capitalist measures modify this setup.)

In a classic communist style structure, if you ask the head of a large manufacturer how much money the company makes, he has no answer. He can only tell you about his assignment, how well he meets the quota, and the schedule. Without marketplace accountability, neither consumer demand nor quality enters into his consideration; instead, producing required statistical results determines his decisions.

Consequently, management accepts bad work from its employees. Then because of shoddy production, leaders can convince workers they need government for supervision and provision. Yury Orlov, a Russian physicist, wrote these words in an exported, underground article: "The dictatorship finds it useful if the average citizen has a certain complex of guilt and gratitude for being treated leniently." By giving permission to do bad work the Party keeps workers happy in spite of the system's failures. By such tactics the Party controls, says Mikhail Heller *(Cogs in the Wheel: the formation of the Soviet man).*

Because the economy is politicized, gifts and favors (bribery) pay for goods and services. Dishonesty becomes a way of life. Corruption is "not a passing aberration," writes Philip Short *(The Dragon and the Bear),* "but is intrinsic to the way the system is ordered." "Corruption," he says, "becomes part of the currency of daily life, a lubricant that must be constantly applied just to get anything done."

Enabling each other to exchange favors according to access to goods through government jobs, the Party from top to bottom, rewards big, middle, and small bosses with tiny crumbs of power. Therefore, most fall in line in order to receive the benefits of cooperation. In this way peasants too become part of the bureaucratic machine. Thus even in totalitarianism you find collusion and consent from the masses. This, Hannah Arendt calls "very disquieting."

why so much fuss about Marxism?

Some view poverty as the worst possible condition and look upon those who oppose communism as alarmists. Poverty is the foremost concern for the poor, they say. But is poverty the worst possible evil?

To illustrate this point, consider poverty and its alternatives as suggested by Charles Murray *(In Pursuit: Of Happiness and Good Govern-*

ment): Imagine having to choose between two couples to adopt your child. One choice is a poverty stricken couple of integrity, character, high ideals; they're industrious, unselfish, honest; they value education and will be diligent in training the child. The other choice is a prosperous couple equally affectionate but undisciplined, irresponsible, opportunistic, and indifferent to the education of your child. Which couple would you choose? Does poverty override all other considerations?

Others who deplore talk of a communist menace look on Marxism as a rational social principle even if occasionally brutal. For them it's akin to their way of thinking—that for the sake of progress, groups of people might have to be liquidated. But Marxists go beyond weeding out hostile opponents. History shows they strike at not only potential opponents but also random targets; purging is their means of control.

practice versus promise

The general view of those not alarmed by communism is that, at least, the poor will benefit. For, they say, if you are starving, Marxism is good news. Yes, good news if it delivers what it promises! But it doesn't. History records that communist leaders actually create starvation conditions. And not only by their inefficient economy. Why? To infantilize the citizenry, to make their dependency on government total, Mikhail Heller says. By owning the means of livelihood, he says, communism can withhold subsistence to all who will not submit.

As terrible as are the records of physical abuse, communism's blow at the heart of what is human is even worse, says Jean-Francois Revel. And Milovan Djilas *(The New Class)* agrees. "It would be wrong to think," Djilas writes, "that other forms of discrimination—race, caste, national—are worse than ideological discrimination . . . Other types of discrimination may crush a human being physically, while ideological discrimination strikes at the very thing in the human being which is perhaps most peculiarly his own. Tyranny over the mind is the most complete and most brutal type of tyranny; every other tyranny begins and ends with it. . . [Communists] makes it impossible for any thought other than their own to prevail. Man may renounce much, but he must think and he has a deep need to express his thoughts. It is profoundly sickening to be compelled to remain silent when there is need for expression. It is tyranny at its worst. . . to compel men to express thoughts that are not their own."

Ironically, this movement, which ends in tyranny, begins with high moral principles. Revolutionaries join together, not only because of common ideas and suffering, but also out of selfless love, comradeship, solidarity. Such warm and direct sincerity can be produced only by battles in which men either win or die. Also, between men and women, comradeliness exists with sexless passion, intimacy of thoughts, mutual aid, and frankness. To this Djilas, Lepp, and other one-time Marxists testify. But harsh reality finally brings euphoric idealism to an end.

What's puzzling is why, with all the facts available today about the *end* results of Marxism in history, an intelligent person chooses to embrace communism. The answer may be more psychological than intellectual. For under the guise of the pursuit of high ideals, communism offers the chance to express rebellion against established authority. Subsequent deeper involvement and commitment then lead to rationalization about the betrayal of the original ideals.

Ignace Lepp explains further. When the intellectual commits himself to the Marxist movement, he trades his freedom for a total package. Why he joins communism is unimportant. Once he becomes a member, he accepts without question the party's changing concept of existence. Reversals and betrayals are accepted as steps to their goal. Since "truth" lies in the party, he remains loyal regardless of what happens.

With this unyielding loyalty causing a deaf ear to human cries, enslavement becomes not only total but permanent. Djilas and others write that the system entraps even the ruling elite themselves. It is a closed system, cut off from outsiders. If a leader is accused—for some reason of the state—it's too late for him to integrate himself into any other group even if any were available. He is completely alone. "Man cannot fight or live outside of society," Djilas says. And there is no society outside communism in those countries.

To get a true picture, Revel recommends comparing communist countries not with democratic or capitalist societies only, but with *all* past civilizations. Though many of history's regimes were neither democratic nor totalitarian, they were all living societies that created valuable civilizations. Not so with Marxist regimes. Though other governments may oppress, Revel writes, Marxist ones—in every aspect of their structures—negate that which is human.

Reform efforts that challenge the system itself fail. Milovan Djilas pressed for a two party government in Yugoslavia. And for that he landed first in prison and now in exile. He says that in practice Marxist theory achieves the opposite of what it promises: The state becomes stronger instead of weaker, the standard of living lower, the difference between city and country greater, the gap between intellectual and physical work wider, elitism stronger, and capitalist countries better. Not a single communist regime *achieves* Marxism's great goals, he writes.

the ultimate hidden goal of Marxists

What is the communist aim? Equality? Fraternity? Help for the poor? Djilas, from his vantage point in exile, gives the answer: In spite of promises and high ideals, he says, communists have only one goal; and it is hidden: The real aim of its leaders is *power*.

Communist "power over men is the most complete known to history," Djilas says. Unlike in all other systems, the party has no political overseers, neither masters nor owners. Party members form a new class, which Djilas compares with the old one, in his book, *The New Class*. The party is as greedy as the bourgeoisie, he says, but not as frugal, as exclusive as the aristocracy, but without their ideals and chivalry. To gain and keep *power,* the new class establishes *authority* through party ownership and buttresses power and authority with *ideology*. Power, ownership (authority), and Marxist ideology* are the pillars of the communist state, Djilas writes.

Communists can do away with forced labor camps and mock trials of "spies" and "traitors" if their reason for doing so is for the interest of the State, says Lepp. And they can stop talking about revolution and military expansion—even as they have today—but they will not *renounce* either. They can sacrifice even authority and ideology, says Djilas, but they can't give up power. For even though communism goes through phases, power remains the goal.

*Power, authority, teachings. See pages 142, 146.

Marxism—has it ever been applied?

When all is said about results, modern idealists say, "Marxism has failed because it has never been applied as Marx taught it." Fritz Raddatz, however, says the flaw lies not in execution but in the system itself. Marx's colleague and close friend, Wilhelm Liebknecht recognized this. When he read Marx's *Critique of Political Economy,* he wept because he saw "a central contradiction" in a major premise.* The question Liebknecht asked is, how is labor defrauded? He raised the question because Marx says that under capitalism and in all economies, labor receives in full the value of the labor power that produces use-value. If so, what is Marx's charge, Liebknecht asks. How can Marx claim that labor should receive *more* than its labor value? How can he say labor contributes *all* the surplus value? Liebknecht sees here "a gap in logic." Without a rational explanation, "a mystical attribute" would have to account for labor's production of surplus value.** If Liebknecht is right, Marxist leaders fail in their stated goals, not because of misinterpreting or misimplementing Marxist dogma, but as a result of following those principles and reaping the consequences.

And conversely, the measure of success some communist countries achieve depends upon their modifying a basic Marxist premise. The East Germans are an example. They modified Marxist global education, which promotes an international outlook favoring proletarianism, blurs nation-state boundaries, and discourages national loyalties. In the eighties the East Germans abandoned the Marxist global principle and began to foster national pride. Their latest history books now revive German heroes and establish emotional ties with their pre-Nazi past. They've restored a place in history for even Chancellor Bismarck, who at one time banned socialism, and they've revived protestant theologian Martin Luther. No longer does the government call Luther a "traitor to the peasants"; instead it calls him "an outstanding humanist."

Rudy Koshar, University of Southern California (Insight 3/20/89)

*Marxist Franz Mehring confirms Liebknecht's criticism of Marx's theory of value .
**To understand this section, see Chart 6, *Marxist Principles Defined, page 36.*
Surplus value is the value above that which the laborer earns and receives for his subsistence. From surplus value, the capitalist pays rent, interest, etc., reinvests, and receives profits.

says that though the East German government clings to Marxist central planning and party control, its leaders realize socialism is not enough. In the artificial and nonpermanent status of the invented territorial space of East Germany, they now seek identity not in communism but in their national culture and heritage.

And with the change in policy, citizens respect authority and pull together for a better economy. East Germany leads Marxist European nations in production and technology, says Henry Kamm (New York Times 3/13/89). Kamm quotes a Czechoslovak: "Those _____ Germans. They even make socialism work." Compared to capitalist societies, however, the East German economy lags behind.

England, on the other hand, is an example of a country that suffered the consequences of applying Marxist principles. Harold Laski, a Marxist scholar active in the British Labor Party, attests to the fact that after World War II, England began to build a socialist society based on Marxist ideas. In remarks about the Communist Manifesto in his 1967 book, Laski said that although labor leader Atlee was not a Marxist, "there was not a word in the sentences of [Atlee] that I have quoted which could not have been eagerly accepted by the authors of the Communist Manifesto." In his 1967 book, Laski wrote hopefully, "It is not merely patriotic emotion that makes British socialists feel that here, as nowhere else, the truth of their principles will be tested." He wrote these words before the trial period. He didn't realize that this experiment would bring England's world status and its economy to its lowest ebb. Today, over twenty years later, after she tested those principles and saw them fail, England abandoned the Marxist direction and steadily regains her strength.

If after over a century and a half, *no* good Marxist model exists, where is the evidence Marx's teachings will ever accomplish his goals?

PART C
JESUS

the poem Jesus read at Nazareth
the claim that angered his townspeople

"The Spirit of the Lord God is upon me,

Because the Lord has anointed me

To preach good tidings to the poor;

He has sent me to heal the brokenhearted,

To proclaim liberty to the captives,

And the opening of the prison to those who are bound;

To proclaim the acceptable year of the Lord."

--Isaiah 60:1,2a

Jesus and his times

Except for a reference by Flavius Josephus, a Jewish historian, little is known about Jesus' life apart from scripture and what history and archeology reveal of the times.

Jesus lived from about 5 B.C. to about A.D. 30. At his birth, Israel was a province in the Roman Empire, which at that time ruled 54 million subjects around the Mediterranean, scholars estimate. Of these people, only one in ten enjoyed the rights and duties of citizens. They were united by the official language of Latin although the different peoples spoke many languages within the empire. In Israel, the common people spoke Aramaic, but educated classes in the East communicated in Greek. (Greek is the language of the New Testament.)

Scripture says that after Jesus' birth, his parents offered a sacrifice prescribed for the poor: turtledoves or pigeons. James Kelso in *An Archeologist Looks at the Gospels* describes how the poor of Jesus' day lived. When weather permitted, they utilized outdoor space for living. An oven in front of the house provided the kitchen; there the women baked the chief food of their diet, bread. The flat rooftop served as another outdoor room for use as a storeroom, a place for drying grapes and figs for winter use, and a bedroom for hot weather. The house of the poor would have one room or two, sometimes with an additional room for a family business; in Jesus' case, a carpenter shop.

As a boy Jesus probably attended a synagogue school where he memorized scripture. Because handwritten copies were too expensive, memorization was the way to own a Bible. Also, young Jesus may have cared for sheep for family and for neighbors. In his shepherd work, from the hill above the town, he could see the Carmel headland, Mount Gilboa, the Mediterranean Sea, and other landmarks of ancient Jewish history.

Scripture states that both Jesus and his foster father Joseph were carpenters in their hometown, Nazareth, a small hillside town at the junction of seven crossroads. Carpenters of that day made wooden plows, yokes, threshing sledges, pitchforks, shovels for winnowing, and ox goads. Their job was not to build houses because no Israeli built his house of wood. Their job was to make doors and lattice windows for houses and provide logs for roofs as well as build furniture and cabinets—all of this with a few tools.

The job of carpenters sometimes included felling trees in the forests around Nazareth, transporting them, ripsawing logs to make lumber, and drying wood. If this was part of Jesus' work, he would have had to possess a lot of brute strength. The physical labor of Jesus and Joseph, however, was probably not limited to carpentering. They might also have helped harvest the barley, wheat, grape, and olive crops.

Scripture says that after Jesus left Nazareth, he established Capernaum as the center of his travels during his public ministry, but he owned no property; he slept outdoors or stayed with friends.

his life

JESUS

Jesus was a Jew.

He was, in fact, a practicing Jew as were his twelve disciples. "I was not sent except to the lost sheep of the house of Israel," he said before Israel rejected him. Many forget his ethnicity or never stop to think about it. And yet you cannot understand the life of Jesus apart from Israel and its faith and history.

the key to who Jesus is

Jesus submits to authority, exercises it, upholds it, delegates it. His stance toward authority is the key to who he is. From boyhood to his last day, he isn't on the defensive; he is at rest in his Father. At his final trial in a Gentile court Pilate tried to force him to answer his questions. "Do you not know that I have power to crucify you, and power to release you?" Pilate asked. "You could have no power at all against me," Jesus said, "unless it had been given you from above."

Although the Jews did not understand, Jesus knew who he was. As the Father's Son, he submitted both to God's heavenly authority and to his instituted earthly authority, including scripture, Mosaic Law, Jewish ritual worship, governing authorities, Roman rulers, the law of the land, tax collectors, his teachers, his elders, his parents.

Jewish expectations about the Messiah

Jesus' family, like other Jews of their day, did not understand that Messiah* would come first to be crucified and return later to rule forever. Mary and Joseph expected him to deliver Israel from the oppressors of their nation. In prophecies they saw only his second coming.

And they overlooked predictions about the suffering servant in Isaiah 53 and some of the Psalms. Instead of recognizing that Messiah is that suffering servant, they interpreted those passages to mean their own

*The word means "anointed one." In Hebrew, "Messiah"; in Greek, "Christ."

suffering as a nation; they called Israel that persecuted one. They were right about Israel enduring much, but they failed to see that Jesus would come and they would reject him.

When first century Jews read Isaiah 53, they didn't see their Messiah on the cross. Isaiah said the Messiah would be "smitten by God and afflicted. . . he was wounded for our transgressions, he was bruised for our iniquities; the chastisement for our peace was upon him, and by his stripes (whip lashes) we are healed. All we like sheep have gone astray; we have turned, every one, to his own way; and the Lord has laid on him the iniquity of us all. He was led as a lamb to the slaughter." Like their kinsmen, Joseph and Mary didn't understand because this picture contradicted the Jewish vision of a king coming in power and glory.

If Joseph and Mary had today's hindsight, they'd know their son came to earth to die. And they'd know Messiah would come not once but twice. They couldn't see this, however, because the two "comings" that scripture predicted merged before their eyes as one, even as two mountain peaks in the distance appear to be one. Little wonder that they saw the Messiah only as the Lion of Judah, the ruling one, because the preponderance of prophetic evidence casts the Messiah in that role.

Again when the angel in the dream told Joseph, "[Jesus] will save his people from their sins," Joseph thought in terms of his own people, the Jews. To him, *his people* could mean only one thing: that Jesus would save *the people of Israel* from their sins. But he didn't know how Messiah was to do this. He surely didn't understand that Jesus would be, not only king, but high priest—that he would mediate before God for the nation, not just for one year's forgiveness as on the Day of Atonement but for forever (see the books of Leviticus and Hebrews). And even less could Joseph understand that Jesus himself would *be* that sacrifice, the lamb of atonement that would have to die. How could Joseph, the foster father, look at his infant son and see him crucified?

under authority

But Jesus knew who he was even in his youth.

Each year Mary and Joseph, as faithful Jews, took him to Jerusalem for the Feast of the Passover. Traveling home in the pilgrimage crowd of friends, they did not worry about the whereabouts of their trustwor-

thy twelve year old. But after three days, they realized he was missing.
Finally, in the temple they found Jesus, surrounded by teachers and
others astonished by his understanding and the depth of his questions.

"Why have you done this to us?" Mary and Joseph asked Jesus.

"Why were you looking for me?" Jesus asked. "Didn't you know I
must be about my Father's business?" He knew God was his Father.

Jesus respected all those in authority. He obeyed not only his heavenly Father but his earthly parents. The Bible says "he went down
with them and came to Nazareth, and was subject to them."[12]

Paul, author of much of the New Testament, says Jesus was born
"under the Law." To identify with those under its curse, Jesus placed
himself under that scriptural Law even though he declares himself its
fulfillment. When accused of breaking the sabbath, Jesus declared his
sovereignty over the law by saying he is "Lord of the Sabbath." Albeit,
he came not to abolish the Law, the Bible says, but to deliver from its
bondage and to raise it to higher ground.

For others too, Jesus emphasized the importance of submission to
the authority of the Law. In his account of the rich man and Lazarus,
the rich man in torment in Hades begged Abraham to send a messenger
from the dead to his five brothers to warn them, but Abraham said,
"They have the law and the prophets; let them hear them." And he said,
"No, Father Abraham; but if one goes to them from the dead, they will
repent." But Abraham said to him, "If they do not hear Moses and the
prophets, neither will they be persuaded though one rise from the dead."
Jesus considered the Old Testament Law to be sufficient warning.

Jesus commended those who recognized authority. The centurion
who wanted Jesus to heal his servant said that Jesus need not come but
only to speak the word of authority and his servant would be healed. As
a leader of soldiers, this man understood what authority can accomplish.
And for this ability to apply the principle of submission to authority in
the realm of faith, Jesus commended the centurion, and he healed his
servant.

Jesus said unless you submit to earthly lines of authority, you will
not be able to receive authority and power in the spiritual realm. "If you
have not been faithful in what is another man's," he said, "who will

give you what is your own?"[13]

Luke 12:42,43 repeats that message: "Who then is that faithful and wise steward, whom his master will make ruler over his household, to give them their portion of food in due season? Blessed is that servant whom his master will find so doing when he comes." Here Jesus says faithful submission to ordained, earthly authority brings blessing when he, the master, returns.

exercise of authority, display of power

Jesus, under the Law, submitted to its authority. But he also exercised authority with power. When he healed Peter's mother-in-law, he *rebuked* the fever. When the disciples cried out to him because of the storm at sea, he *rebuked* the wind and the raging waters. When he met the demonic in the country of the Gadarenes, he *commanded* the legion of demons to come out of the man. The demons recognized authority and called Jesus the Son of the Most High God. When they begged not to go out into the abyss, he *gave them permission* to enter the herd of swine, which they did. The pigs then ran into the lake and drowned.

Another time, after being accused of breaking the sabbath for eating grain in the fields, Jesus confounded his adversaries by *a demonstration of authority* through a miraculous healing of a man in the synagogue.

And Jesus *conquered* death itself. When he entered the room of the dead daughter of a ruler of a synagogue, he took the girl by the hand and told her. "Little girl, arise." And her spirit returned and she arose immediately. In another instance in the Bible, Lazarus had been dead four days when Jesus called him to come out of the tomb. And Lazarus came.

Even the manner with which Jesus spoke commanded authority. His presence inspired men at a word to leave everything and follow him. His boldness bewildered his enemies; and the common folk took note of their reaction: "They say nothing to him. Do the rulers know indeed that this is truly the Christ?"[14] When officers commissioned to take Jesus into custody returned empty handed, their only explanation was, "No man ever spoke like this man!"[15] Later, more dramatically, in the garden of Gethsemane, all Jesus had to say to his rough, armed captors was "I am he."[16] And his word caused them to draw back and fall to the ground, the Bible says.

delegation of authority

This authority and power Jesus gave to his followers for them to speak and act in his name. When the seventy returned from their mission, they said, "Lord, even the demons are subject to us in your name." And Jesus said, "Behold, I give you the authority to trample on serpents and scorpions, and over all the power of the enemy (Satan)."[17]

challenges to authority

The chief priests and scribes questioned Jesus' authority to cast out moneychangers from the temple. In response to the challenge, Jesus asked about the authority of John the Baptist. "Was it from heaven or from men?"[18] he asked. He had his accusers cornered because if they said from men, the crowd would stone them. On the other hand, they didn't want to acknowledge that John the Baptist was a *bona fide* prophet. So they answered they didn't know. "Neither will I tell you by what authority I do these things," Jesus said.

By his ability to sort out lines of authority, Jesus confounded his adversaries. When they laid a trap for him by asking if it was lawful to pay taxes to Caesar, he asked whose image was on the denarius. It was Caesar's picture. "Render therefore to Caesar the things that are Caesar's," Jesus said, "and to God the things that are God's."[19]

Jesus didn't teach his followers to challenge authority; he didn't say, "Question authority!" as today's bumper stickers advise. But he did at times question *people* in authority, as when he responded to the high priest who asked about his doctrine. "Why do you ask me?" Jesus said. "Ask those who have heard me what I said to them. Indeed they know what I said." Then an officer hit Jesus, saying, "Do you answer the high priest like that?" "If I have spoken evil," Jesus said, "bear witness of the evil; but if well, why do you strike me?"[20] Though Jesus rebuked *people* in authority, he didn't question the authority of the office itself.

scriptural authority

Often when Jewish adversaries challenged the authority of Jesus, he countered with scripture. "You search the scriptures, for in them you think you have eternal life," Jesus told them one time, "and these are they which testify of me. For if you believed Moses, you would believe me; for he wrote about me."[21]

And with believers, too, Jesus grounded his authority in scripture. To two of them, who did not recognize him after his resurrection, Jesus showed the design of their Jewish scriptures—their unity in him, the central character: "And beginning at Moses and all the Prophets, he expounded to them in all the scriptures the things concerning himself."[22]

This understanding of Jesus' place in the Old Testament, the apostle Paul calls the "revelation of the mystery."[23] Like a document with invisible writing held to heat, the not-yet-visible message of Jesus in the Old Testament became readily apparent in New Testament times. It was there all the time.

And how did Jesus triumph in his ultimate tests? By the authority of quoted scripture. Thus with scripture he overcame Satan's temptations when the Holy Spirit led him into the wilderness.[24]

And thus with scripture Jesus overcame on the cross, to which the Holy Spirit led him. At the cross, even Jesus' cry of agony was scripture from Psalm 22: "My God, my God, why have you forsaken me?" By this shout, the Bible says Jesus expressed excruciating pain under the weight of every person's guilt. By this shout he also called followers to take heart, for this cry pointed them to Psalm 22, which has other predictions about his crucifixion: "All my bones are out of joint . . . For dogs (Gentiles) have surrounded me . . . They pierced (nailed) my hands and my feet. . .They divide my garments among them, and for my clothing they cast lots." Finally, by this shout, Jesus pointed his followers to the Psalm's resounding victory: "You have answered me. . . For the kingdom is the Lord's, and he rules over all nations.[25]

relational authority

Jesus' fulfillment of centuries-old Bible prophecies along with his miracles and the purity of his life attest to the broad, sweeping authority he claimed to have. Yet not because of perfect manhood did Jesus have this authority. No, the denial of his self-life made it possible for him moment by moment to live and walk in the Holy Spirit, Jesus says. "The Son," he says, "can do nothing of himself, but what he sees the Father do; for whatever he does, the Son also does in like manner."[26] By this he testified wherein his perfection lay: in his utter dependence. The gospel of John, in particular, pictures relational authority.

John in the first chapter establishes Jesus as God and in later chapters*
shows his interdependent oneness with God the Father and God the
Holy Spirit. Scripture pictures a man whose authority rests, above all,
in his submission to and expression of the authority of his Father.

ministry

All the ministry of Jesus focuses forward to the crucifixion. He began his journey toward that cross the day he submitted himself to John
the Baptist to baptize him in the river Jordan. John called Jews to
repentance. So when Jesus asked to be baptized, John was puzzled. "I
have need to be baptized by you, and are you coming to me?" he asked.

Earlier John had told the crowd about the coming Messiah by saying, "I indeed baptize you with water unto repentance, but he who is
coming after me is mightier than I, whose sandals I am not worthy to
carry. He will baptize you with the Holy Spirit and fire."[27]

But John at this moment didn't know Jesus was the Messiah. After
all, as boys he and Jesus probably played together (though of different
tribes, their mothers were related). Probably what caused him to remon-
strate about baptizing Jesus was his firsthand knowledge of the irre-
proachable character of Jesus' life.

To John's question about why he should baptize him, Jesus had an
answer. "Permit it to be so now, for thus it is fitting for us to fulfill all
righteousness."[28] With this act, by submitting to the hands that put
him under the waters of the Jordan, Jesus signified his willingness to
submit to the crucifixion that lay ahead. Going down he identified himself with sinners in their death, and coming up, the Bible says he led
the way out of death and hell for those who identify with him. Before
he took one step into his public ministry, Jesus counted the cost. He
saw the difficulties that lay ahead; he knew his mission and accepted it.

About three years later, what Jesus accepted by faith at baptism
approached the point of fulfillment. At that time he rode on a donkey
through the cheering throngs of Jerusalem for a short moment of recognition as Messiah King. This popular acclaim sealed his fate. The leaders knew they had to act quickly to accomplish Jesus' death because the
populace wanted to crown him king . "Rejoice greatly, O daughter of

*This relationship found in chapters 12 through 17 of the gospel of John.

Zion!" the prophet Zechariah prophesied hundreds of years before. "Behold your King is coming to you. . . lowly and riding on a donkey, a colt."[29]

The people had followed Jesus from place to place to see him, to hear him speak, and to watch him heal the sick, raise the dead, cast out demons, and perform miracles. Always "the common people heard him gladly."[30]

But a week later the same crowds that hailed Jesus as King, cried "Crucify him! Crucify him!" Pilate, the Roman procurator, declared Jesus innocent[31] and tried to release him—because he knew the leaders accused Jesus "because of envy."[32] But with each plea Pilate made, the crowd yelled more loudly, "Crucify him! Crucify him! We have no king but Caesar."

The crowd's cry was born not from their knowledge of Jesus and his healings, his provision, his love, and his miracles. Rather the cry erupted from the protracted plotting of enemies in high places, who incited the masses to a lynching spirit.[33] At this point even Jesus' chosen twelve forsook him. This was the hour that the powers of darkness prevailed. But not for long.

Later how the disciples rejoiced! For after Jesus' crucifixion, he appeared to them in his resurrected body. And what a comfort when Jesus breathed on them and said, "Receive the Holy Spirit!"[34] For at that moment, scriptures say, the disciples became the first to be born from above, as Jesus had promised.[35] All others before had known God only through his anointed external instruments, but now these had his Spirit indwelling them.

Jesus appeared in his glorified body not just to his disciples but to five hundred men at once.[36] Years later many of these men still lived, the apostle Paul said in his letter to the church in Corinth. As eye witnesses the five hundred no doubt told the good news everywhere they went and thus authenticated the resurrection. For if Jesus rose from the dead as he promised, listeners believed he would fulfill the other part of his promise: to resurrect all believers from the dead in the future.

By seeing Jesus in his new body, those believers could see the kind of body they expected to have after their resurrection. They touched him, watched him eat fish, and saw him suddenly appear behind the locked doors of their meetingplaces.

But forty days after his resurrection, something even more startling happened. The Bible says that Jesus without any external means of locomotion began to rise into the sky. The disciples watched in amazement. "Men of Galilee," two men in white apparel told them, "why do you stand gazing up into heaven? This same Jesus, who was taken up from you into heaven, will so come in like manner as you saw him go into heaven."[37]

During Jesus' life, several times he had foretold his death, his resurrection, and that he would go to be with his Father. He even referred to his journey skyward,[38] but his followers had been unable to comprehend. Later, however, after Jesus breathed his life into them,[39] they became Christians. And with his Spirit living within them, when they recalled what he said and did, they understood.

authority today

Before Jesus departed, he told his disciples, "All authority has been given to me in heaven and on earth. Go, therefore. . ." And the Bible says he commanded them to be his witnesses by supernatural power.[40]

His life and its authority Jesus plants in his people. This you find in his manifesto: *"A farmer went out to sow his seed."*

his manifesto

JESUS
INTRODUCTORY REMARKS
Matthew 13

the manifesto—from the old to the new

The Bible presents a drama in which the life and spirit of the new covenant intersects with the letter of the old Israeli one. The resultant tremors shake the foundations of the pillars of society, the leaders. And they in their terror focus on Jesus as the earth-shaker they fear. They close in for the kill.

At this point Jesus gathers his followers to explain—in story form without handles for his enemies to grab—his heretofore hidden plan. This is his manifesto. With this blueprint, Jesus prepares his followers for the transition from the old to the new, for relational change, for regrouping. He unveils mysteries hidden in his listeners' past and opens their eyes to see and understand the future.

the old

Of those in Jesus' audience, most live under the Mosaic covenant. They see all others, the Gentiles, as being outside God's people; that is, except for the ones who join the nation of Israel.

This crowd of people know their past. For they have been careful to pass down their religious traditions from generation to generation. They know that God called Abraham out of idol worship because he wanted to reveal himself to mankind. From this one man came their nation, Israel. And from this nation was to come another man, the Messiah, to set up his kingdom forever.

From Abraham to Jesus, the ancestors of these Jews related to God through his anointed instruments—through the holy scriptures, through the rituals and blood sacrifices of Jewish temple worship, and through men who ministered—judges, prophets, priests, and kings. Under the Mosaic Law these intermediaries linked man to God.

the new

Now Jesus changes that. In his manifesto he eliminates the need for intermediaries and ends national exclusiveness. Instead he offers direct access to his Father in heaven. After his resurrection, by his Spirit Jesus will indwell believers. And he will plant his people everywhere.

With his offer of a new relationship with God, a regrouping of peoples takes place. Whereas before scriptures classified believers and unbelievers as Jews or Gentiles respectively, now Jesus distinguishes the redeemed from the lost as those who accept or reject him.

the kingdom—in historical context

That's the big picture. Now let's return to the immediate historical context. Jesus has spread the good news: The kingdom promised in Hebrew scripture is ready to begin. Though the common people hear him gladly, leaders fear the power that Jesus will gain through his popularity. When they hear the message of repentance, if they feel conviction in their hearts, they do not yield to it. Instead they plot Jesus' demise.

At this point of rejection, Jesus announces his startling manifesto: God will reveal himself to the world in a new way—not through the witness of one nation, Israel, but through the witness of individual Christians scattered everywhere.

the kingdom—delayed by a new order

Because of Israel's rejection, Jesus shifts gears and prepares for a delay of Israel's kingdom. In his manifesto, he shows these first Jewish Christians what to expect in the interim. He introduces a new order.

the kingdom—open to all

While Jesus talks to the crowds about these things, his mother and brothers request his audience. They're seeking to rescue him from his foolishness because they think he is "out of his mind".[41] Jesus' response to their summons is, "Who is my mother and who are my brothers?. . . Here are my mother and my brothers! For whoever does the will of my Father in heaven is my brother and sister and mother."

In this turning away from his nuclear family's misconception about who he is, he illustrates his turning away from his greater Jewish family, Israel. With the Jewish leaders plotting his destruction, this is a turning point. Jesus accepts Israel's rejection, turns to the Gentiles, and invites them. He enlarges his circle. Now he welcomes *anyone* who is willing to join his "family."

The broadness of his invitation accords with the promise to Abraham that through him and his posterity all nations will be blessed.[42] Jesus' followers, however, do not yet understand his sacrificial death nor what it is to accomplish.

the kingdom—for Israel, the church age parenthetical

Nevertheless, even with regrouping, Jesus still sees the Jews as one of three biblical groups: Jews, Christians, unbelievers.[43]

Just ahead lies the church age of believers and unbelievers according to their acceptance or rejection of Jesus. The Jews who accept Jesus become part of the church. For the rest as a whole, the church age will be a parenthetical period suspended in Jewish history. During this period, many individual living Jews will not recognize Jesus as the king for whom they wait.

Moses predicted this parenthetical Gentile period: "I will provoke [Israel] to jealousy by those who are not a nation."[44] Because the Jews overlooked this scripture, Paul in the New Testament calls the hidden truth a mystery or a secret. He explains it in the light of history's development: "Through [the Jews'] fall, to provoke them to jealousy, salvation has come to the Gentiles."[45] Paul says that neither Jews nor Gentiles deserve God's mercy. Nevertheless, through the waywardness of both people groups, God will display his grace. For one day "all Israel will be saved," the Bible says.[46]

the kingdom—bad news, good news

In Matthew 13 Jesus is ready to speak to a huge crowd, one so big and so enraptured by him that he has to get into a boat to keep from being mobbed. With enemies circling round and waiting for an opportunity to strike, Jesus gives his plan in symbolic story form. He speaks in parables. With this approach, his opponents, because of their hard hearts, cannot comprehend.*

Jesus' followers, conversely, are eager to hear and understand and

---

*Jesus in his manifesto correlates a hard heart and lack of understanding. These enemies, however, cannot help but recognize obvious allusions to themselves.

will do anything to press closer to hear. They're grateful for the door
open before them and long for the kingdom of which he speaks. And
they're willing to see and understand. What they don't comprehend, they
can ponder until future events and knowledge of scripture dovetail to unlock their meaning. The stories are so simple they are easy to recall.

the kingdom—pictured in parables

Simple as the parables are, interpretations vary. As for this writer, I
used to look at these parables as little lessons exhorting the reader to
shape up in certain ways. But I now attach greater significance to them
because I recognize their strategic placement and their importance in
defining the kingdom of which Jesus speaks. Jesus himself underlines
their importance when he refers to the introductory story, the parable of
the sower, by saying, "Do you not understand this parable? How then
will you understand all the parables?"[47] Isn't that a thought worth pon-
dering? that the parable of the sower unlocks all of Jesus' parables, not
just the ones in Matthew 13? and that they are interrelated?

When I look for the significance of the parables in the greater context of the whole Bible, my understanding opens up. First, I recognize
the parables as pivotal between the two covenants. They link the old
covenant with the new and open up the interpretation of both. Second, I
find significance when I sort out the Bible's three people groups—Jews,
Christians, unbelievers. For I know I'll stay on target only if I correctly
apply my knowledge of their roles in the drama as a whole.

When I look for significance in the lesser context of the four gospels and within the manifesto itself, I find clues to word-picture mean-
ings: the farmer, the mustard seed, birds, yeast, and others. Looking for
clues in other parables lines up with Jesus' emphasis on the interrela-
tedness of the parables.

Finally, when I look at the context within each parable, how I focus
makes a difference. For instance, in the parable of the sower, I need to
ask, who is the main character? (The farmer.) And what is his purpose?
(To harvest a crop.) Jesus himself makes this point when he calls this
the parable of the sower, not the parable of the soils or the parable of
the seeds. The focus is important because it affects the interpretation.

These thoughts set the stage for the first reading of Jesus' manifesto.

THE MANIFESTO OF JESUS
BIBLICAL TEXT OF MATTHEW 13 (NIV)

the parable of the sower

That same day Jesus went out of the house and sat by the lake. [2]Such large crowds gathered around him that he got into a boat and sat in it, while all the people stood on the shore. [3]Then he told them many things in parables, saying: "A farmer went out to sow his seed. [4]As he was scattering the seed, some fell along the path, and the birds came and ate it up. [5]Some fell on rocky places, where it did not have much soil. It sprang up quickly, because the soil was shallow. [6]But when the sun came up, the plants were scorched, and they withered because they had no root. [7]Other seed fell among thorns, which grew up and choked the plants. [8]Still other seed fell on good soil, where it produced a crop—a hundred, sixty or thirty times what was sown. [9]He who has ears, let him hear."

understanding the parables

[10]The disciples came to him and asked, "Why do you speak to the people in parables?"

[11]He replied, "The knowledge of the secrets of the kingdom of heaven has been given to you, but not to them. [12]Whoever has will be given more, and he will have an abundance. Whoever does not have, even what he has will be taken from him. [13]This is why I speak to them in parables:

"Though seeing, they do not see;
though hearing, they do not hear or understand.

[14]In them is fulfilled the prophecy of Isaiah:

"'You will be ever hearing but never understanding;
you will be ever seeing but never perceiving.
[15]For this people's heart has become calloused;
they hardly hear with their ears,
and they have closed their eyes.

Otherwise they might see with their eyes,
   hear with their ears,
   understand with their hearts
   and turn, and I would heal them.'"
16But blessed are your eyes because they see, and your ears because they
hear. 17For I tell you the truth, many prophets and righteous men longed
to see what you see but did not see it, and to hear what you hear but did
not hear it.

the parable of the sower explained
   18"Listen then to what the parable of the sower means: 19When anyone hears the message about the kingdom and does not understand it, the
evil one comes and snatches away what was sown in his heart. This is
the seed sown along the path. 20What was sown on rocky places is the
man who hears the word and at once receives it with joy. 21But since he
has no root, he lasts only a short time. When trouble or persecution
comes because of the word, he quickly falls away. 22What was sown
among the thorns is the man who hears the word, but the worries of this
life and the deceitfulness of wealth choke it, making it unfruitful. 23But
what was sown on good soil is the man who hears the word and understands it. He produces a crop, yielding a hundred, sixty or thirty times
what was sown."

the parable of the weeds
   24Jesus told them another parable: "The kingdom of heaven is like a
man who sowed good seed in his field. 25But while everyone was sleeping, his enemy came and sowed weeds among the wheat, and went away.
26When the wheat sprouted and formed heads, then the weeds also
appeared.
   27"The owner's servants came to him and said, 'Sir, didn't you sow
good seed in your field? Where then did the weeds come from?'
   28"'An enemy did this,' he replied.
   "The servants asked him, 'Do you want us to go and pull them up?'
   29"'No,' he answered, 'because while you are pulling the weeds, you
may root up the wheat with them. 30Let both grow together until the
harvest. At that time I will tell the harvesters: First collect the weeds and
tie them in bundles to be burned, then gather the wheat and bring it into
my barn.'"

the parables of the mustard seed and the yeast
31He told them another parable: "The kingdom of heaven is like a mustard seed, which a man took and planted in his field. 32Though it is the smallest of all your seeds, yet when it grows, it is the largest of garden plants and becomes a tree, so that the birds of the air come and perch in its branches."

33He told them still another parable: "The kingdom of heaven is like yeast that a woman took and mixed into a large amount of flour until it worked all through the dough."

mysteries revealed and prophecy fulfilled
34Jesus spoke all these things to the crowd in parables; he did not say anything to them without using a parable. 35So was fulfilled what was spoken through the prophet:

"I will open my mouth in parables,
I will utter things hidden since the creation of the world."

the parable of the weeds explained
36Then he left the crowd and went into the house. His disciples came to him and said, "Explain to us the parable of the weeds in the field."

37He answered, "The one who sowed the good seed is the Son of Man. 38The field is the world, and the good seed stands for the sons of the kingdom. The weeds are the sons of the evil one, 39and the enemy who sows them is the devil. The harvest is the end of the age, and the harvesters are angels.

40"As the weeds are pulled up and burned in the fire, so it will be at the end of the age. 41The Son of Man will send out his angels, and they will weed out of his kingdom everything that causes sin and all who do evil. 42They will throw them into the fiery furnace, where there will be weeping and gnashing of teeth. 43Then the righteous will shine like the sun in the kingdom of their Father. He who has ears, let him hear.

the parables of the hidden treasure and the pearl
44"The kingdom of heaven is like treasure hidden in a field. When a man found it, he hid it again, and then in his joy went and sold all he had and bought that field.

45"Again, the kingdom of heaven is like a merchant looking for fine pearls. 46When he found one of great value, he went away and sold everything he had and bought it.

the parable of the net
47"Once again, the kingdom of heaven is like a net that was let down into the lake and caught all kinds of fish. 48When it was full, the fishermen pulled it up on the shore. Then they sat down and collected the good fish in baskets, but threw the bad away. 49This is how it will be at the end of the age. The angels will come and separate the wicked from the righteous 50and throw them into the fiery furnace, where there will be weeping and gnashing of teeth."

51"Have you understood all these things?" Jesus asked.

"Yes," they replied.

52He said to them, "Therefore every teacher of the law who has been instructed about the kingdom of heaven is like the owner of a house who brings out of his storeroom new treasures as well as old."

a prophet without honor
53When Jesus had finished these parables, he moved on from there. 54Coming to his home town, he began teaching the people in their synagogue, and they were amazed. "Where did this man get this wisdom and these miraculous powers?" they asked. 55"Isn't this the carpenter's son? Isn't his mother's name Mary, and aren't his brothers James, Joseph, Simon and Judas? 56Aren't all his sisters with us? Where then did this man get all these things?" 57And they took offense at him.

But Jesus said to them, "Only in his home town and in his own house is a prophet without honor."

58And he did not do many miracles there because of their lack of faith.

THREE-PART
COMMENTARY ON
THE MANIFESTO OF JESUS
Matthew 13

PART ONE—THE NEW ORDER

You Are the Message, says the title of a recent book; your words are
meaningless unless the rest of you is in synchronization. So writes author Roger Ailes, media coach to the Great Communicator Ronald Rea-
gan. "Everything you do in relation to other people," Ailes says,
"causes them to make judgments about what you stand for and what
your message is."

In his manifesto, Jesus too says, "You are the message." In the parable of the sower, Jesus says his followers are his word to the world.

Jesus and the believer
the believer and the world

parable of the sower

*That same day Jesus went out of the house and sat by the lake. [2]Such
large crowds gathered around him that he got into a boat and sat in it,
while all the people stood on the shore. [3]Then he told them many things
in parables, saying: "A farmer went out to sow his seed. [4]As he was scattering the seed, some fell along the path, and the birds came and ate it
up. [5]Some fell on rocky places, where it did not have much soil. It
sprang up quickly, because the soil was shallow. [6]But when the sun came
up, the plants were scorched, and they withered because they had no root.
[7]Other seed fell among thorns, which grew up and choked the plants.
[8]Still other seed fell on good soil, where it produced a crop—a hundred,
sixty or thirty times what was sown. [9]He who has ears, let him hear."*

"A farmer went out to sow his seed."

In that first sentence of the parable of the sower, you meet the main
character and learn that his purpose is to sow seed. The question is, who
is the farmer and what is the seed he is planting?

Remember that other parables and scriptures give clues for understanding the parables. In the parable of the weeds, Jesus identifies the

farmer: "He who sows the good seed is the Son of Man (the Messiah)."* And in the same parable, he identifies the field: "The field is the world."

Four sources reveal the symbolism of the seed:
1) Parable of the weeds, Matthew 13: "The seeds are sons of the kingdom."
2) Parable of the sower, Matthew 13: "What was sown. . . is the man."**
3) Parable of the sower, Luke 8:11: "The seed is the word of God."
4) John 1:1,14: Jesus is the Word of God.
Conclusion: Seeds are people in whom Jesus the Word lives.
              They are Christians.

Now for the parable of the sower, combine the identities: Jesus (the farmer) plants Christians (his seeds) in the world (field). From this planting, he will reap a worldwide harvest at the end of the age.

the parable of the sower explained

18"Listen then to what the parable of the sower means: 19When anyone hears the message about the kingdom and does not understand it, the evil one comes and snatches away what was sown in his heart. This is the seed sown along the path. 20What was sown on rocky places is the man who hears the word and at once receives it with joy. 21But since he has no root, he lasts only a short time. When trouble or persecution comes because of the word, he quickly falls away. 22What was sown among the thorns is the man who hears the word, but the worries of this life and the deceitfulness of wealth choke it, making it unfruitful. 23But what was sown on good soil is the man who hears the word and understands it. He produces a crop, yielding a hundred, sixty or thirty times what was sown."

the kind of planting

What kind of crop is this parable talking about? Not the fruitfulness of a vine and its branches, as in John 15. In that illustration, the sap flows from the vine to impart its life to the fruit-bearing branches.

*Son of Man, an Old Testament title for the Messiah, is the title Jesus most often uses to refer to himself.
**NIV here gives a good, close literal translation of the Greek. You can check that with Nestle Greek text of *Interlinear Greek English New Testament.* Zondervan

There the vine and branches portray how the indwelling Spirit of Christ works through the life of believers to produce the fruits of the Spirit: love, joy, peace, and more.[48] That is the fruitfulness produced in the character and born of inner communion.

The fruitfulness of the parable of the sower, on the other hand, speaks not of inner growth but of outer ministry. Here the seed is an entity separate from the sower. It dies to itself. And it reproduces. Through God's planted people, others come into the kingdom. This is the fruitfulness of witness.

the measure of the planting

Jesus plants his people. Some will have no witness because the enemy will snatch away the seed before it germinates. Some will spring up for only a short time and have little witness. Some will have a wider witness but will yield only part of their potential. Some, however, will yield a bountiful witness: one seed producing a hundred seeds, or one seed producing sixty others, or one producing thirty. In other words, some seeds accomplish the sower's purpose; others do not; some do partially. The seed fulfills the farmer's purpose by the measure of its crop.

This parable says, therefore, that if you're a Christian, you will either change the environment for God or the environment will change you for the worse. It follows from the illustration of this parable that the only way you can change the world around you is *to be the message*. Therefore, the measure you care about the message that you portray is the measure God can use you.

the value of the planted

To illustrate this principle, let's look at a key moment in the life of Dr. James Dobson, popular Christian radio psychologist of *Family Focus*. After the early success of his book, *Dare to Discipline*, Dr. Dobson walked through the aisles of the huge book convention where his book was gaining attention. In the exhiliration of such acclaim, the young author felt a tug from God calling him aside to tell him, "You will have the power to hurt many people." A sobering thought! With that word, the doctor turned away from the pride of accomplishment to face the responsibility that accompanies it. At that moment he faced the fact that *he had something priceless to guard: his testimony.*

Dr. Dobson is a public figure, but isn't every Christian a leader? Yes, Jesus in his manifesto implies that if you're a Christian, you're a leader whether you realize it or not. Your life and words either build or destroy. Other Christians follow you. And the world watches you.

The manifesto says if you're a Christian, you're the means by which God reveals himself to others: *You are the message.* The awesome conclusion about this privilege is that if God entrusts you with his name, that means you have power to honor him or disgrace him by what you express. It also means that the price you are willing to pay to stand up to be counted is the measure of your estimation of this sacred trust.

the life-germ of the planted

But you can't treasure and guard your testimony unless you know its value. That requires understanding. In this parable Jesus says understanding is the life-germ of fruitfulness. The one who has no understanding—the first seed—lacks what is vital; he has no testimony and cannot fulfill God's purpose in his life. For without understanding of the kingdom, he can do no good for God's cause. Conversely, the one who is fruitful—the last seed—accomplishes God's purpose through his life; he is the one who understands the message, Jesus says. The degree of understanding, therefore, determines the measure of appreciation and nurture of Jesus' supernatural life and, consequently, its multiplication in the lives of others.

King Solomon centuries before connects understanding to knowing God: "Knowledge of the Holy One is understanding."[49] And he adds that illumination comes from God, that a believer is only a light-holder: "The spirit of a man is the lamp of the Lord."[50] Therefore, if you're a Christian, you need to avoid that which would hide that light from the view of others."*Let* your light so shine before men," Jesus says, "that they may see your good works and glorify your Father in heaven."[51]

the purpose of the planting

In both Mark 4 and Luke 8 immediately after the parable of the sower, Jesus asks questions that prompt examination of purpose and meaning for life. "Is a lamp brought to be put under a basket or under a bed?" he asks. "Is it not to be set on a lampstand?"[52] "You are the light of the world," he continues. These little word pictures add weight to the message of the parable of the sower. And they show how ridiculous it is for a Christian to hide who he is.

Throughout the Matthew manifesto, Jesus talks about life, understanding, and light. The thrust of what he says is that he plants his life to be lived out and his light to shine out. And that spark of life and light does not have to struggle for expression.

Life doesn't strain to express itself or to reproduce its life-nature. A cat does not try to be a cat nor does a tiger try to be a tiger. A cat *is* a cat. A tiger *is* a tiger. And a Christian *is* a Christian. And each reproduces itself as part of the natural process. In this parable Jesus says if you're a Christian you don't need more trying to be one, but you do need more understanding if you are to allow that life full rein.

And light doesn't try to shine; it just shines. If you have the light of understanding, that light shines. Yet you can hide it. The question Jesus asks is "What sense does it make to thwart your reason for being? Why keep the world in the dark?"

What is Jesus saying about why he put you here? He says he put you here to be his person. That's all. And for the rest of his ministry, that is the gist of Jesus' message: "Be my person." Even in his very last words to his disciples, he repeated it this way: "You shall be witnesses to me."[53]

Do you see why understanding this parable is important for understanding the others? How can you understand the rest of Jesus' plan if you don't understand the parable that states his purpose for the new order? God will now reveal himself to the world not through one nation but through his people planted everywhere.

understanding the parables

After Jesus told the parable of the sower and before he explained it, he clued in the crowd about the field of reference in which he intended for it to be understood. In the following passage, he presents fulfilled Jewish prophecies, which predicted that the hidden mysteries of early times would one day be revealed.

10The disciples came to him and asked, "Why do you speak to the people in parables?"

11He replied, "The knowledge of the secrets of the kingdom of heav-

en has been given to you, but not to them. 12Whoever has will be given
more, and he will have an abundance. Whoever does not have, even what
he has will be taken from him. 13This is why I speak to them in
parables:

> *"Though seeing, they do not see;*
> *though hearing, they do not hear or understand.*

14In them is fulfilled the prophecy of Isaiah:

> *"'You will be ever hearing but never understanding;*
> *you will be ever seeing but never perceiving.*
> *15For this people's heart has become calloused;*
> *they hardly hear with their ears,*
> *and they have closed their eyes.*
> *Otherwise they might see with their eyes,*
> *hear with their ears,*
> *understand with their hearts*
> *and turn, and I would heal them.'"*

16But blessed are your eyes because they see, and your ears because they
hear. 17For I tell you the truth, many prophets and righteous men longed
to see what you see but did not see it, and to hear what you hear but did
not hear it.

Jesus tells his contemporaries how fortunate they are to fathom
secrets their forefathers longed to unlock but could not. He encourages
openness to his message and warns against callousness, because hardheartedness hinders understanding, he says. He adds that the greater the
understanding, the greater the capacity to receive. *"Whoever has will be*
given more, and he will have an abundance. Whoever does not have,
even what he has will be taken from him." The process of understanding is dynamic, not static. It is either progressive or regressive, compar-
able to the use or lack of use of a muscle. Use or lose, Jesus says.

And later in the chapter, Jesus once again refers to the unveiling of
the hidden and to the fulfilling of prophecy from Psalm 78:2:

> *35So was fulfilled what was spoken through the prophet:*
> *I will open my mouth in parables,*
> *I will utter things hidden since the creation of the world ."*

What in the parables has been hidden until this time? The new order:

the church. Though not comprehended in Old Testament times, the new order nonetheless fulfills what the prophets spoke. Also hidden until this revelation of the church is the delay of the kingdom in Israel.

This church age is part of the larger period, the kingdom of heaven, the timeframe with which Jesus' manifesto deals. The kingdom of heaven is that interim period from the time Jesus lived on earth to the time he rids his kingdom of evil.

PART TWO—THE KINGDOM OF HEAVEN IS LIKE. . .
A TIME OF CONFLICT, A MIX OF GOOD AND EVIL (six parables)
what is the kingdom of heaven?

Marx in his manifesto deals with a period of time from his day to the time the state withers away and ushers in a new society. He calls that time period *the communist movement.* Jesus in his manifesto deals with a period of time from his day to the time he sets up his eternal kingdom. He calls that time period *the kingdom of heaven.*

Within his designated timeframe, each man—in telling his plan and purpose in a manifesto—deals with the relationship of groups of people, Marx during the days of the communist movement and Jesus during the days of the kingdom of heaven. Marx talks about proletarians, the bourgeois, and aristocrats. Jesus talks about the church, the Jews, and unbelievers. Marx describes the "struggle" between the proletariat and the bourgeoisie. Jesus describes the conflict between his kingdom and Satan's.

To announce a new order, Jesus begins his manifesto with "A farmer went out to sow his seed." He pictures himself planting Christians to be his scattered witnesses. The lifetime of this new people group on earth is the *church age,* an inserted time period, which for Israel postpones the setting up of their Messianic kingdom. This interim of delay is a hiatus in Hebrew history.

The next six parables in the manifesto begin with "The kingdom of heaven is like. . ." "The kingdom of heaven" is a phrase you find only in the book of Matthew, the book written specifically to the Jews to help them understand the transition period between the old covenant and the new. And because "the kingdom of heaven" appears so frequently in the manifesto, you have to understand it to understand Jesus' outline of the future.

One key to understanding the phrase is to know that Jesus in his manifesto leaves no doubt that this time period is a mixture of good and evil, a time when Satan and his followers combat Jesus and his people.

Another key to understanding the kingdom of heaven is to determine the literal translation, which is *the kingdom of heavens.** That will be the term used hereafter in this discussion.

The vital key to understanding the kingdom of heavens is to know that these (atmospheric) heavens harbor battling forces. The opponents battle for the hearts of men on earth, but the headquarters for both sides are above, in the heavens. Yes, God and his hosts are not the only ones there; Satan and his cohorts also work out their strategies and dispatch their messengers from above the battlefield.**

As stated earlier, *the kingdom of heavens* is a time interval, a time of conflict between good and evil. It is to be distinguished from the other two timeframes in the New Testament—*the kingdom of God* and *the church age*. Though sometimes one phrase substitutes for the other, the terms are not universally interchangeable.+

The context of the New Testament, confirmed by hints in the Old Testament, reveals that the three time blocks fit inside each other like children's nesting blocks (Figure 2). We live today in the church age. And since it is the smallest time block, it nests inside the other two blocks. That means that the present time lies within all three realms.

Let's examine each time block. First, the biggest block of time is *the kingdom of God* block. Within it are the other two time blocks, the kingdom of heavens and the church age. The kingdom of God is eternal. Besides encompassing the two smaller blocks of time with their present good-and-evil mixture, the kingdom of God began before time

*See Literal English Translation of Nestle Greek text of *The* Interlinear Greek-English New Testament. Zondervan.

**Ephesians 6:12 says the devil has "spiritual hosts of wickedness in heavenly places." Revelation 20:10 says the heavens will harbor battling forces until Satan is cast to the earth, bound, and finally thrown in the lake of fire.

+To illustrate how this can be, you can say, "All horses are animals," but you cannot say, "All animals are horses" because you are dealing with categories and subcategories. Though you can substitute "animals" for "horses, sometimes you cannot do the reverse.

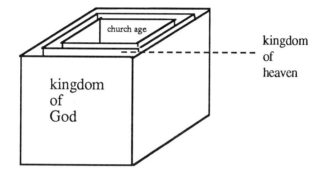

Figure 2: NESTED TIME BLOCKS OF THE NEW TESTAMENT

and extends into perfect infinity when there will be no more evil.

Second, *the kingdom of heavens* time block fits inside the kingdom of God block. And the smallest time block, the church age fits inside the kingdom of heavens block. For the Jews, the kingdom of heavens began before the church age and extends beyond that timeframe and on through the endtimes and man's final judgment. *The kingdom of heavens began in Jesus' day and ends after he rids the world of all evil.*

Third, *the church age* is the smallest time block. It fits inside the kingdom of heavens. The church age began after Jesus' resurrection and will end when he returns to gather living Christians to heaven. Yes, the church age will one day end even though the church itself (Christians) will live forever.

Jesus and Satan; Jesus and believers
Satan and his people
believers and Satan's people; judgment of both

parable of the weeds

24Jesus told them another parable: "The kingdom of heaven is like a man who sowed good seed in his field. 25But while everyone was sleeping, his enemy came and sowed weeds among the wheat, and went away. 26When the wheat sprouted and formed heads, then the weeds also appeared.

27"The owner's servants came to him and said, 'Sir, didn't you sow good seed in your field? Where then did the weeds come from?'

28"'An enemy did this,' he replied.

"The servants asked him, 'Do you want us to go and pull them up?'

29"'No,' he answered, 'because while you are pulling the weeds, you may root up the wheat with them. 30Let both grow together until the harvest. At that time I will tell the harvesters: First collect the weeds and tie them in bundles to be burned, then gather the wheat and bring it into my barn.'"

the parable of the weeds explained

36Then he left the crowd and went into the house. His disciples came to him and said, "Explain to us the parable of the weeds in the field."

37He answered, "The one who sowed the good seed is the Son of Man. 38The field is the world, and the good seed stands for the sons of the kingdom. The weeds are the sons of the evil one, 39and the enemy who sows them is the devil. The harvest is the end of the age, and the harvesters are angels.

40"As the weeds are pulled up and burned in the fire, so it will be at the end of the age. 41The Son of Man will send out his angels, and they will weed out of his kingdom everything that causes sin and all who do evil. 42They will throw them into the fiery furnace, where there will be weeping and gnashing of teeth. 43Then the righteous will shine like the sun in the kingdom of their Father. He who has ears, let him hear.

This parable pictures the conflict between Satan and Jesus. In it their followers grow up together on earth until the final judgment.

The field is not the church; it's the world, Jesus says. In the world believers and unbelievers will live together until the end. He does not say, therefore, that the church should not purge or discipline its membership. He, in fact, at another time, specifies how the church should deal with wrongdoers in its ranks.[54]

This parable helps the believer—the Jewish believer of Jesus' day or the Christian since Jesus' resurrection—face injustice. Only if you are confident that in due time justice will prevail will you be able to withhold judgment and make wise, not vengeful, decisions. For you will remember that God said, "Vengeance is mine." If you know this, you can rest content in the hands of the just judge who can distinguish the good from the bad.

Also, this parable tells the believer what to expect. If you know Satan will continue his presence and activity in this world through his followers, then, if you're a believer, you'll be prepared to deal with God's enemies and their deceptions. You won't go off on wrong tangents.

And this parable will not allow the believer to be misled by world planners that promise to eliminate war by social or political measures or by the improvement of unregenerate men. For if you're a believer, you will seek peace and pursue it but not to the point of discarding God-given convictions. Neither will you endorse utopian ideas. This parable teaches that Satan's followers will operate until the Son of Man rules the earth. If that's true, that means there can be no lasting world peace until the Prince of Peace returns.

the church, its growth, and Satan's workers;
the nation of Israel, its development
                                    parable of the mustard seed
                                    and parable of the yeast (leaven)

The crowd Jesus addresses is Jewish. Some of them accept him as Messiah or Christ and will form the church after his departure. Others in the crowd will follow their leaders in rejecting him. In these parallel parables of the mustard seed and the yeast, Jesus contrasts the future of these two groups of his listeners: the church and Israel.

For historical background, the first church begins as a sect in Judaism. For about forty years Christian Jews worship as a sect in the Jewish temple and synagogues until their full rejection by the nation's leaders about A.D. 70, the time of the destruction of the temple by Roman armies. Not until their ouster do Jesus' followers become an entity separate from Judaism.

a) parable of the mustard seed

31He told them another parable: "The kingdom of heaven is like a mustard seed, which a man took and planted in his field. 32Though it is the smallest of all your seeds, yet when it grows, it is the largest of garden plants and becomes a tree, so that the birds of the air come and perch in its branches."

The parable of the mustard seed illustrates the birth and growth of the church. According to previous clues, the man is Jesus, the field is the world, and the mustard seed is the mustard seed of faith. The clue for the identity of the mustard seed lies in this statement by Jesus: "If you have faith as a mustard seed, you will say to this mountain, 'Move from here to there,' and it will move; and nothing will be impossible for you."[55]

The mustard seed of faith is the beginning point of the church. When Jesus asked Peter who he thought Jesus was, Peter replied, "You are the Christ, the Son of the living God." "Flesh and blood has not revealed this to you," Jesus said, "but my Father who is in heaven. . . On this rock, I will build my church, and the gates of Hades shall not prevail against it."[56] Here Jesus says he will build his church on the kind of faith Peter exhibited. This faith implanted by God in a believer is as small as a mustard seed in its inception, but it is destined to grow into a large tree—not into the tree as an organization but into the tree as *a living organism.* New Testament writers say this living church is made up of all who have supernatural life through Jesus.

The figure of the seed speaks of life and of the tininess of faith in its beginning. The figure of the tree speaks of the unity of the church's community life in its growth and maturity. And the figure of the birds perched in its shade[57] speaks of evil emissaries from Satan, who will associate themselves with the church. (You can infer the symbolic meaning of the birds from the parable of the sower.)

The birds are not part of the tree; they only lurk in its branches. These birds cannot penetrate the internal life of the tree, the church of this parable. These enemies "shall not prevail against" the church. Adversaries can infiltrate church organizations, but apart from becoming true believers themselves, they cannot integrate into the living tree.

And so Jesus assures his listeners that though the beginning of the church would be inconspicuous, the church will grow, will flourish, and will mature "to the measure of the stature of the fullness of Christ."[58]

b) parable of the yeast (leaven)

33He told them still another parable: "The kingdom of heaven is like yeast that a woman took and mixed into a large amount (literally translated, three measures) *of flour until it worked all through the dough."*

The Old Testament represents leaven as a symbol of evil and excludes it from Jewish sacrifices foreshadowing the coming Messiah.* In the New Testament, Jesus also depicts leaven as evil. He warns about the leaven of the Pharisees and scribes (their hypocrisy and legalism), the leaven of the Sadducees (their discrediting of the supernatural), and the leaven of Herod (his antichristian abuse of political power).

This parable is the second of a pair. This repetition of the same theme two different ways indicates a possible parallel to be searched out. A look at the church and Israel shows that their comparison fits the parallel of this parable pair. They are similar in that the parable of the mustard seed pictures the growth and development of the church, and this parable of the leaven pictures the growth and development of Israel.

They differ in a couple of ways. First, they have different starting points. The parable of the mustard seed points to a beginning of the church *during* the kingdom of heavens whereas this parable illustrates a continuation of Israel, which began *before* the time of the kingdom of heavens. Second, they have different representations of evil. In the parable of the mustard seed, evil rests in the branches and is *external*. In this parable, evil (leaven) works inside the dough and is *internal*.

One clue that Israel is the subject intended in the parable of the leaven is that the symbol of leaven is a Jewish symbol, as already pointed

*Leaven in the Leviticus 3 peace offering is an exception because it typifies the imperfection of the offerer.

out. Another clue is a phrase that describes a Jewish sacrifice offered by significant biblical characters. The offering is *three measures of meal* (in NKJ).* In Genesis 18 Abraham and Sarah entertained three important personages, who may have represented the Lord himself. For the guests Abraham had Sarah prepare three measures of meal into bread. Again the same phrase, three measures of meal, appears in the account about the sacrificial offerings of Gideon and still later of Hannah before Samuel's birth.[59] In Israel's early days, to leaven fresh dough for baking, the housewife used a small lump saved from a previous batch. In a similar, self-propagating way, God guaranteed Israel's survival. For no matter how unfaithful the nation, he always preserved a remnant to carry forward his purpose for them. But with the preserved legacy, the remnant transmitted something else, the Bible says: the leaven of sin. Beginning with Adam, they passed it on from one generation to the next.

Into this tainted stream of humanity God intervened. Jesus came. He entered humanity without an earthly father and without the leaven of sin, and yet he was born under the Law, the Bible says. Subsequently, on the cross he *became sin* for those he represented under the curse of the law. Jesus was the final remnant of Israel under the old covenant because all forsook him—even those closest to him, his twelve Jewish disciples. And thus his deserting followers, by identifying with his slayers, left Jesus as the last remnant of Israel.

In his resurrection Jesus is the beginning dough of a new covenant: a new lump without leaven, free from sin.[60] Henceforth by identification with Jesus in his death, anyone can become part of that new lump. For Paul writes: "Purge out the old leaven that you may be a new lump . . . For indeed Christ, our Passover, was sacrificed for us."

But Israel, as a nation under its leaders, didn't accept, as from God, Jesus' offer of the kingdom; it rejected him and continued in the old lump leavened by sin. And so if Jesus truly was the Messiah that God sent to his own nation, the development of apostasy—the abandonment of God in his will—pictured by this parable fits. A little leaven leavens the whole lump. But rather than dwell on the negative, let's go quickly to the next pair of parables to see how precious Israel is to God.

*An ephah equals 3 measures of flour in I Samuel 1:24 and Judges 6:19.

Jesus and Israel
Jesus and the church

parable of the hidden treasure and
parable of the pearl of great value

This pair of parables, the second of a double pair of small parables, pictures redemption. And so again we search out the parallel intended. If the previous pair pictures Israel and the church, then this pair about the treasure and the pearl may parallel the same two people groups in order to show something different.

What differs is perspective. In the first pair of parables about the mustard seed and the leaven, man sees the church and Israel from his limited viewpoint; that is, in the symbolism of the birds and the leaven, man sees evil mixed in with the good. In this second pair of parables about the treasure and the pearl, on the other hand, Jesus speaks from his Father's perspective: He sees the end result. He sees only the beauty and wonder of the Jewish people and the church, both his very own. His viewpoint is not circumscribed and is unchanging.

a) parable of the hidden treasure

44 "The kingdom of heaven is like treasure hidden in a field. When a man found it, he hid it again, and then in his joy went and sold all he had and bought that field.

who is the treasure?

This parable of the treasure pictures redemption of a hidden treasure. Past clues reveal that the man is Jesus and the field is the world. The question is in the identity of the treasure. And because the parable pictures Jesus as the redeemer-person, the question must be not *what* but *who* is his treasure?

Israel still on God's agenda

Israel is that treasure. Scriptures show that God has for the land of Israel a place in his heart and a plan for her future. "You shall be a special treasure to me above all people," God says of Israel, "for all the earth is mine. And you shall be to me a kingdom of priests and a holy nation."[61] Also, scriptures say, "For the Lord has chosen Jacob for himself, Israel for his special treasure."[62] Though some translations use words other than *treasure*, they all picture Israel prized by God as his very own.

Israel and the land inseparable

The Bible closely associates Israel with its land. Biblical prophecies about Israel's restoration to the promised land abound. Therefore, serious Bible readers predicted the modern miracle of the 1948 restoration of Israel as a nation. But most scriptural prophecies speak of a yet future date when Israel will reign on the earth in a kingdom without end: "And the days of your mourning shall be ended. Also your people shall all be righteous; they *shall inherit the land forever*, the branch of my planting, the work of my hands."[63]

Israel hidden

Israel is a treasure buried in the world's field. Its people, hidden in Abraham, were recognized only by God, who called Abraham to father a nation. The Israeli were hidden while the Gentile nations ruled over them. And they were hidden over the centuries during their dispersal throughout many lands. Today though a nation, they are still hidden as God's spiritual people. They have no temple in which to practice their faith. And they fight just for ethnic survival. Israel is still hidden because she has not yet come into her own.

Israel redeemed?

Jesus came to earth to redeem his treasure Israel. "I was not sent except to the lost sheep of the house of Israel," he said.[64] He came for his treasure but Israel rejected him; he couldn't buy his treasure without buying the field in which it was hidden. He had to redeem the world.

Israel a joy

To buy that field was a joy to Jesus.*"In his joy"* the man went and sold all he had. Jesus rejoiced in paying the price on the cross because by that act, he bought the field in which his treasure lay. Here and elsewhere the Bible associates joy with the land of Israel. The Psalmist calls Jerusalem *"the joy of the whole earth."*[65]. . . . "For he remembered his holy promise, and Abraham his servant. *He brought out his people with joy*, his chosen ones with gladness. He *gave them the lands* of the Gentiles."[66]

From his Father's perspective, Jesus looks at Israel and sees the people in their future, purified state as the Old Testament prophet predicted: "I will cleanse them from all their iniquity. . . then [Israel] shall be to me *a name of joy, a praise, and an honor before all nations of the earth*, who shall hear all the good that I do to them."[67] Jesus saw beyond his rejection by Israel to his fulfillment of joy in Israel to whom he came. In the New Testament the author of the letter to the Hebrews says to run the race, "looking unto Jesus, the author and finisher of our faith, who *for the joy* that was set before him endured the cross."[68]

In the scope of this book, these scriptures are not intended to prove a point about this parable but to invite an open mind while reading the context of the whole Bible. As you read keep in mind the three groups in Jewish scriptures—Jews, Gentiles, unbelievers—and the three groups in the New Testament—Jews, the church, unbelievers. You will see that the Bible deals with Israel throughout. It talks over and over again of Israel's future eternal glory under the Messiah.

Jesus sold all because of joy for his treasure hidden in Israel and for the field in which it lies. For this treasure hidden yet, some day Jesus will return.

b) parable of the pearl of great value

45"Again, the kingdom of heaven is like a merchant looking for fine pearls. 46When he found one of great value, he went away and sold everything he had and bought it.

This second parable repeats the theme of the first: A man finds something valuable and sells everything he has to redeem it. And it raises the same question as its parallel partner: Who is the treasured one? Also like the parable of the treasure, this one pictures God's viewpoint: He sees not a mixture of good and evil but priceless beauty in his people—in this instance, the church.

One distinction about this parable is that the man, Jesus, plays a slightly different role. He is a merchant, a gem dealer, a businessman; a venture capitalist, if you will: In plying his trade, he risks all that he owns to make this investment.

Another distinction about this parable is that the man is actively looking for this pearl. In the parallel parable about Israel, the man is not seeking for treasure; he discovers it hidden in a field. About the

church, Paul quotes Isaiah: "I was found by those who did not seek me
. . . to a nation that was not called by my name (Gentiles—the
church)."[69] This age of mercy opens the door to outcasts—the formerly
excluded Gentiles and those ostracized for other reasons. To Zaccheus,
the despised tax collector for the Roman rulers, Jesus said, "the Son of
Man has come *to seek* and to save that which was lost."[70]

A final distinction about the parable of the pearl is that Jesus does
not hide his discovery. Before he left the earth, he commissioned his
disciples to go into the world to preach good news. He openly displays
the beauty of his gem and excludes no one from sharing in its glory.

For this priceless pearl and for his treasure in the field, Jesus will
one day return. He paid the price for his people, the Bible says. He will
claim them for his own.

Jesus and unbelievers in the judgment
parable of the net

[47]*"Once again, the kingdom of heaven is like a net that was let down
into the lake and caught all kinds of fish.* [48]*When it was full, the fishermen pulled it up on the shore. Then they sat down and collected the good
fish in baskets, but threw the bad away.* [49]*This is how it will be at the
end of the age. The angels will come and separate the wicked from the
righteous* [50]*and throw them into the fiery furnace, where there will be
weeping and gnashing of teeth."*

The previous double twin parables picture Israel and the church.
This parable showcases a third people group, unbelievers. It is also one
of a pair even though the two are not presented side by side. This parable of the net parallels the parable of the weeds. Both paint the picture
of the gathering in of believers and the casting into the fiery furnace of
the unbelievers. The difference between the two parables is in viewpoint. The parable of the weeds illustrates man's viewpoint: that is,
while good and bad grow up together, man sees injustice. The parable
of the net illustrates God's viewpoint. All he sees is the end when his
own justice prevails. The parable of the weeds like the parables of the
mustard seed and the leaven shows man's viewpoint. The parable of the
net like the parables of the treasure and the pearl shows God's viewpoint.

Also, there is another parallel. Of these six kingdom of heaven parables, the first and the last are the parable of the weeds and the parable of the net. Sandwiched between are the two little pair-sets about Israel and the church. Using a sandwich as an analogy, the bread contrasts with the filling: The unbelievers in the weeds and the net parables contrast with believers—Israel and the church—in the twin pair-sets.

PART THREE—UNDERSTANDING, A STUDY IN CONTRASTS
WILLING TO UNDERSTAND
the believer and two covenants: Jesus binds old to new
51"Have you understood all these things?" Jesus asked.
"Yes," they replied.
52He said to them, "Therefore every teacher of the law who has been instructed about the kingdom of heaven is like the owner of a house who brings out of his storeroom new treasures as well as old."

Jesus concludes by emphasizing, as he has throughout the manifesto, the importance of being willing to understand. He says if his disciples understand his teachings, they have access to all that is precious in the old and new covenants and can minister from them to the needs of the household of faith.

Jesus opens the door to a vault of treasures, new and old. Out of Israel has come the church: Out of the justice of the old covenant springs the grace of the new. The apostle Paul says that Jewish law was a schoolmaster to teach man his condition before God and that Jesus came to satisfy its righteous demands. In Jesus the two covenants meet. For to behold him is to behold the Father's glory, "full of grace and truth (justice),"[71] the apostle John says. "Mercy and truth (justice) have met together," the Old Testament says. "Righteousness and peace have kissed each other. Truth shall spring out of the earth, and righteousness shall look down from heaven."[72] Jesus binds the old to the new.

UNWILLING TO UNDERSTAND
afterword
53When Jesus had finished these parables, he moved on from there.
54Coming to his home town, he began teaching the people in their synagogue, and they were amazed. "Where did this man get this wisdom and

these miraculous powers?" they asked. 55*"Isn't this the carpenter's son?*

Isn't his mother's name Mary, and aren't his brothers James, Joseph, Simon and Judas?

56*Aren't all his sisters with us? Where then did this man get all these things?"* 57*And they took offense at him.*

But Jesus said to them, "Only in his home town and in his own house is a prophet without honor."

58*And he did not do many miracles there because of their lack of faith.*

After Jesus finished laying out his manifesto, he went to his hometown, Nazareth. And because his fellow citizens could not accept his extraordinary ministry, he "did not do many miracles there." Luke says that when Jesus, in the synagogue, applied to himself Isaiah's prophecy about the Messiah, the townspeople could not accept him as the fulfillment of that ancient prophecy. They became enraged and tried to lynch him.[73] Like some of the lakeside listeners, these Nazarenes had not ears to hear nor eyes to see. Like Marxists, instead of an open hand to receive, theirs was the closed fist salute of anger, clinched in power. To escape, Jesus walked right through the crowds and left them to seethe in their chosen bitterness.

Here Jesus demonstrates his respect for individual choice: "He did not do many miracles there because of their lack of faith." In this incident, Jesus lives up to the ideal with which famed David Livingston endows him; that is, although Jesus allows consequences of choice—both natural and judgmental—to follow their course, he does not force himself or his message on anyone. He simply invites. He is as Livingston describes him: "Jesus is a gentleman."

He is the message and so are his followers.

CHART 10
Jesus' manifesto in a capsule (Matthew 13)

1. To reap a harvest Jesus plants his people everywhere.
   Their witness for God replaces Israel's national witness.

2. Jesus' life is to be lived out, his light to shine out.
   His people are his message to the world.

3. Understanding is the vital key to fulfilling his purpose.
   Hardheartedness and unbelief prevent understanding.
   Willingness is necessary.

4. The new order, the church, will begin, grow, and thrive.

5. Israel's kingdom is delayed by her unbelief and by the new order.

6. The present, the kingdom of heaven, is a time of conflict.
   Satan and his followers fight but will lose.

7. Jesus sees believers as precious.
   He redeems his people and will return for them.

8. Good and evil will exist until the final judgment.

9. Then unbelievers will be judged.

10. Jesus will reign and peace, harmony, and justice will prevail.

eight

his targeted enemies

JESUS HATES SIN AND SATAN

sin defined

Jesus hates sin and Satan, its author.

He speaks more of sin and its consequences and the fate of Satan and unforgiven sinners than almost anyone else in the Bible. He exposed the hypocrisy of the leaders of his day and blasted unbelief wherever he found it. Before Jesus presented his manifesto, he called the leaders "this wicked generation." Later he pronounced woes upon them. "Serpents, brood of vipers! How can you escape the condemnation of hell?" he asked.

In the temple one day, Jesus targeted sin. With a whip made of cords, he stormed in, poured out the changers' money, turned over their tables, and drove out before him the moneychangers and their sheep, cattle, and doves. "Take these things away!" he demanded. "Do not make my Father's house a house of merchandise."[74] He may have snapped the whip to grab their attention—the Bible doesn't say—but he probably didn't have to lay a hand on anyone; most likely, all cowered before his anger.

And why would they cower? Because they knew they were wrong. They came face to face with the truth. "My house shall be called a house of prayer for all nations.[75] But you have made it a den of thieves,"[76] Jesus quoted. As always, he struck at the heart of the matter by bringing the participants back to basics, to purpose and meaning. He showed them they were missing the mark.

Missing the mark is literally what the word *sin* means. Sin means acting apart from the will of God. And acting apart from the will of God is the foundation stone of what Marx teaches. For Marx there is no God to obey, no conviction of sin—only evolving economic structures set up to facilitate the forward march of nature, science, and history. For Marx his aim is to hit his own mark, not God's.

rebellion, the root problem
"Missing the mark" for God begins in rebellion. And it is universal, the Bible says. Marx, therefore, in his plan to overthrow existing social institutions has no difficulty in finding and exploiting rebellious instincts in the hearts of malcontents. To Marx, sin is not against God but against society, not personal but corporate and political. To him sin is to resist revolution.

Whereas Marx loves to rebel, Jesus hates rebellion. He believes "the earth is the Lord's and all its fullness, the world and those who dwell therein."[77] He constantly declares his submission to his Father. He relates personally to the Father and offers a personal relationship to any who follow him. Unlike Marx, Jesus does not identify evil by social institutions but by individual response to his Father and to himself. One by one, not en masse, he confronts sin. He did this when the angry crowd charged the adulterous woman. "He who is without sin among you, let him throw a stone at her first," Jesus says.

Jesus by his example upholds what the New Testament teaches, that God ordains government and law for society's good.[78] But in this, Jesus neither endorses collaboration with evil leaders nor disobedience to God's Word. On the contrary, history records that he inspires courage to oppose totalitarianism.

Talk of such submission to authority, especially to earthly authority, has a strange sound to modern ears. It conjures up images of robots blindly following Nazi demagogues. Therefore, American Christians raise two questions about applying these principles to practical living.

(1) *Are citizens to collaborate with totalitarian dictatorships?* Of course Christians cannot support totalitarianism. Obeying the law, however, is not evil, the Bible says, for the law prohibits antisocial behavior and criminal activity. Therefore, to obey the law, even in a communist land is not to side with evil but is to uphold the general good; the law offers protection and order in place of chaos.

Jesus, through Paul, teaches submission to the state because no authority exists except that appointed by God, he says. The apostle Paul in one passage says to "render therefore to all their due"[79] and also to "owe no one anything except to love." And so, for Jesus and his people, love and submission to authority go hand in hand. For only love makes a proper basis for submission (even as hate aimed at the bourgeois motivates rebellion for Marxists). On this bedrock of love and submission, Jesus sums up all his commands: First, love God. Second, love your neighbor as yourself.

(2) *Should citizens cooperate with enemies of God's Word?* Though Christians uphold the law, scripture allows an exception. If your own government forbids you to proclaim what you believe, how can you respond except like Peter and John in a similar situation: "Whether it is right in the sight of God to listen to you more than to God, you judge. For we cannot but speak the things which we have seen and heard."[80]

heart motivation, the crux

For Jesus, motivation is what counts. With the motivation of love, you can accomplish God's will. Without the motivation of love, you "miss the mark"; you sin. And sin Jesus hates. Even if you give all your goods to feed the poor but have not love, it is nothing, Jesus' apostle writes.[81] Marx, on the other hand, believes that to change the economic framework of society is to change the individual. *For Marx, not heart motivation but social arrangement is what counts.*

Heart motivation, says Jesus' manifesto, changes not only individual lives for good or ill but also influences others in society. In politics the kind of influence depends upon the motivation of the leadership. For example, the motivation of the French and Russian revolutions created quite different results from those of the American Revolution.

Applying the criteria of Dr. Hannah Arendt, Irving Kristol of New York University calls the French and Russian revolutions "rebellions." Mob passion, irresponsible desire, disdain for authority distinguish such uprisings. And they do not accomplish their aims. "A rebellion is more a sociological event than a political action," writes Kristol. A rebellious spirit sweeps everything along and ends up being a revolution betrayed.

Famed French historian, Francois Furet, comments about the aborted efforts of the French Revolution: "Today when I write, I try to see what was already there in 1789 that became incompatible with liberty in 1793." If Furet looked at the motivating spirit of rebellion, he might find his answer. For what can rebellion do but destabilize? It cannot create the environment democracy and a good economy require. How can such a society long remain free?

The American Revolution, in contrast, ushered in the first democratic republic in history and brought about beneficial and lasting change. Seeking redress for specific wrongs, Americans made reasonable demands. Instead of expressing a will-to-power like Russian revolutionists, Americans sought to circumscribe power. Aware that republics had failed over the centuries, Americans armed themselves with knowledge of reasons for failure in the past. They embodied this knowledge in *The Federalist*. They approached their task with trepidation and made innovations with great anxiety. Their object was to bring political institutions in line with already proven, American self-governing practices. Generally, these sober minded Americans—with a history of respect for law, order, and independent governance—were reluctant to take up arms.

Even if today's Americans don't make distinctions between types of revolution, Soviet Union's Mikhail Gorbachev does. In his 1988 speech before the United Nations, he cited only two great revolutions—the French Revolution and the Russian Revolution. In spite of his desire to win the sympathy of Americans, Gorbachev didn't mention the American Revolution because he too distinguishes it from the other two.

Discovery of rebellion and hate as sources of Marxist motivation led former American Marxist David Horowitz to write a radical friend to ask him to examine what he believes "because it is a mirror of the dark center of the radical heart: not compassion, but resentment. . . not the longing for justice, but the desire for revenge; not a quest for peace, but a call to arms. It is war that feeds the true radical passions, which are not altruism and love, but nihilism and hate." According to this statement by a man who once espoused that cause, the goal of *a manmade utopia* is achieved through hate, resentment, and revenge. These sins, Jesus hates.

greed, covetousness, and trust in riches condemned

Jesus condemns sin in all its forms, including greed, covetousness, and trust in riches. Instead he proffers love for the believer's guide even in his use of material possessions. And because the Bible says that God entrusts wealth for responsible stewardship for *his* honor and glory, Jesus does not equate wealth and exploitation as does Marx. Jesus, in fact, endorses the biblical portrayal of wealth as God's blessing. Through his apostle, however, Jesus warns "not to be haughty, nor to trust in uncertain riches but in the living God, who gives us richly all things to enjoy."[82] To a rich young ruler, for one, Jesus gave the command to sell all, give to the poor, and follow him.[83]

But Jesus nowhere makes a universal indictment of riches. Rather he warns against confidence in wealth because it prevents release of faith in God. He always looks at the heart. "For out of the heart proceed evil thoughts, murders, adulteries, fornications, thefts, false witness, blasphemies. These are the things which defile a man,"[84] Jesus says.

Although Jesus targets the human heart, not social structures, as the brewing pot for evil, still he warns against oppression of the poor. For this too he hates. "Indeed the wages of the laborers who mowed your fields," says a New Testament writer, "which you kept back by fraud, cry out; and the cries of the reapers have reached the ears of the Lord."[85] In condemning oppression, Jesus is "no respecter of persons" or classes. For everyone—capitalist and Marxist alike—he says stealing from the poor results from the heart's greed and covetousness.

Jesus believes "the laborer is worthy of his wages."[86] And through Paul, he commands masters to give their servants what is just and fair, in the sure knowledge that they too have a Master in heaven to whom they are accountable.[87]

armed burglars climb walls

Marx, like Jesus, preaches to the poor. He too promises change for a better life, but he fails to deliver. About the sinful motivation of such leadership, Jesus cautions: "He who does not enter the sheepfold by the door but climbs up some other way," he says, "the same is a thief and a robber. . . The thief does not come except to steal, and to kill, and to destroy." Jesus points to the door as the proper entry. "I am the door," he says. But Marx does not listen; he climbs the wall and enjoins others to follow. He shouts to the downtrodden: "Revolt! Steal the reins of power. This will solve all your problems."

Yet the track record proves otherwise.

his influence

JESUS

a world without Jesus?

Have you ever thought about a world without Jesus? George Orwell describes such a world in his book *1984*. Communist countries today might have become just like Oceania, a fictitious nation in *1984*, except that Orwell failed to take into account one thing—Jesus' influence.

In China something altogether different has happened: In place of the hollow men of the novel, *1984*, Chinese Christians risk their lives to tell others about Jesus. And the sparks fire up millions. The millions are a small percentage of the population of more than a billion but many times the number of Christians before communist rule.

In Orwell's book, atheist Winston Smith struggles to remain "human." Because he fails in his resistance to the dehumanizing process, he ends up loving Big Brother, Oceania's bigger-than-life mythic leader, the symbolic embodiment of the totalitarian government.

O'Brien, the torturer in charge of bringing Smith to the "sanity" of a good party member alternates cruelty with kindness. Smith, during one of O'Brien's kinder moments, felt it did not matter to him if O'Brien was a friend or enemy. What mattered was that he was a person he could talk to. "Perhaps," Orwell writes, "one did not want to be loved so much as to be understood. O'Brien had tortured him to the edge of lunacy, and in a little while, it was certain, he would send him to his death. It made no difference. In some sense that went deeper than friendship, they were intimates; somewhere or other, although the actual words might never be spoken, there was a place where they could meet and talk. O'Brien was looking down at him with an expression which suggested that the same thought might be in his own mind."

After instilling distrust by its network spying, Big Brother exploited Smith's acute pain of alienation, which the system itself had created.

a world with Jesus' influence

In the real world, however, because Jesus does influence, such antichristian movements fail in their ultimate objectives even when they accomplish their shortterm goals. To illustrate, let's go back to another antichristian thrust in 1900 in Taiyuan, Shanxi, China.* Before communism existed, a group of foreign Christians suffered intense persecution. Their courage, however, won the heart of an eminent Chinese scholar, who watched them face brutality and murder. Though this slaughter of fifty-nine Catholic and Protestant missionaries was horrendous, not one victim panicked. Not one cried for mercy. All remained serene. Missionary Jonathan Goforth tells the story in *By My Spirit.*

In the courtyard, the scholar listened to a thirteen year old, blond girl who stood before the governor. "Why are you planning to kill us?" she asked. "Haven't our doctors come from far-off lands to give their lives for your people? Many with hopeless diseases have been healed; some who were blind have received their sight. And health and happiness have been brought into thousands of your homes because of what our doctors have done. Is it because of this good that has been done that you are going to kill us?" The governor's head was down. He had nothing to say.

"Governor, you talk a lot about filial piety. It is your claim, is it not, that among the hundred virtues filial piety takes the highest place. But you have hundreds of young men in this province who are opium sots and gamblers. Can they exercise filial piety? Can they love their parents and obey their will? Our missionaries have come from foreign lands and have preached Jesus to them. And he has saved them and given them power to live rightly and to love and obey their parents. Is it then, perhaps, because of this good that has been done that we are to be killed?"

Still the governor bowed his head. Then the drama stopped short. A soldier grasped the girl's hair. With one blow of his sword, he severed her head from her body. And as the scholar watched, a mother quietly instructed her little boy. Then a soldier struck her down. The little fellow stood and waited without a whimper before he too went down.

Afterward the observing scholar asks if it is any wonder that the for-

*The author taught English in Taiyuan in 1984/85.

titude of these Christians should compel him to search the Bible and come to believe that it is in very truth the Word of God. The longterm results of the testimony of those Christians are still being reaped in China today.

These people were committed Christians. But the crisis of facing death sometimes brings others to consider following Jesus' footsteps. For—these seekers ask—who else makes footprints beyond a loved one's grave? These thoughts the apostle Peter expressed when he said to Jesus, "Lord, to whom shall we go? You have the words of eternal life."[88] He could have said it this way: How can we find meaning here and now unless our path is going somewhere—and it's for the long haul?

This longer look keeps followers of Jesus "on target" in crisis. And it also carries other Christians through daily frustrations and disappointments. Just by their daily living, the actions of these quiet people speak so loudly that they change the world around them.

Brother Lawrence, a lay cook in a monastery in the late 1600s, was one of these. A brief record shows he lived out his life in childlike faith. *Daily* he walked in God's presence. By his own testimony we know he had no confidence in his own wisdom and leaned hard on his Master. He just kept his eyes on Jesus and started moving through his day, lifting one foot and then the other. *He* made the footprints, and Jesus did the rest. This means that when Brother Lawrence moved forward against odds, he found power beyond human capacity and rose above the ordinary in ordinary life. By his serenity, he impressed those he served.

Before this lay brother did his tasks, he dedicated each one to God and asked his help. After he finished, he thanked God. When he stumbled, he asked forgiveness and went on as though he had not missed a step. His joy he ascribed to practicing the presence of God. That joy so transformed him that centuries later his life still inspires those who read about a few of his conversations, which others recorded. (See back page.)

influence in history and in social institutions

"Progress" in social spheres does not tell the real story of Jesus' influence. Nevertheless, history records change through "Christian" social movements. But not all the change has been for good. Many things have been carried out in the name of Jesus—including a war called the Crusades, which killed many, including children, and a purge called the Inquisition, which killed the innocent. Some even blame Jesus for Hitler's holocaust by saying Germany was a Christian nation; a 1984 tour guide at a kibbutz in Israel made this bitter charge.

And many great things, too, have been done in the name of Jesus. I could point to beautiful cathedrals and quaint country churches—or to the great artists of the Renaissance: Leonardo Da Vinci, Raphael, Michelangelo, and Benvenuto Cellini.

And in music, how majestic is the Hallelujah chorus in Handel's Messiah! How timeless is Johann Sebastian Bach's music! Bach often wrote *I.N.J.,* for the Latin words meaning *In the Name of Jesus,* on the manuscripts of even his nonreligious works. And Haydn, when asked why his church music was so cheerful, answered, "I cannot make my music otherwise. I write according to the way I feel. When I think upon God, my heart is so full of joy that the notes dance and leap, as it were, from my pen. God has given me a cheerful heart and I cannot help but serve him with a cheerful spirit."*

I could go back to ancient Erasmus, author of one of the first bestsellers. Of him it is said that he laid the egg that hatched Martin Luther and protestantism. Or I could turn in literature to *Paradise Lost* by John Milton, a Christian who studied and lived out Bible teachings. The writer ought himself to be a true poem, he wrote. Like Jesus he was saying, in effect, "You are the message." And John Bunyan. You can't overestimate his influence on the Western world. Next to the Bible his *Pilgrim's Progress* was the most popular book in early America.

Didn't social services originate with Christians? And many continue now in the churches, the Salvation Army, St. Vincent de Paul, YMCA, worldwide food programs for the hungry, and so many others. Also, Christian philanthropists erected libraries, public buildings, charitable institutions. And Christian missionaries—how many Christian hospitals, schools, and colleges were the first hospitals and educational institutions some foreign lands knew?

*Alice Knight, *1001 Stories.*

influence in America

What about early Christian influence in America? Although its impact has been minimized in the public eye in recent years, James Hitchcock says Christian principles inculcated in Americans those virtues needed for self-government *(Whose Values?* Carl Horn, editor). "According to Lawrence Cremin," writes Hitchcock, "the five most popular books during America's first 150 years were religious."

Outsiders also testify to Christian influence in the early United States. In 1831 Alexis de Tocqueville was only twenty-six years old when he traveled around America with a young friend. Though commissioned by the French government to study the prison system of this new country, the two men fulfilled an unofficial mission, too. Tocqueville, for his own satisfaction, wanted to investigate the inner workings of a country that had never known aristocracy. He wanted to discover the essence of democracy. In two volumes of *Democracy in America,* popular then and now, he recorded his conclusions and predictions.

He was impressed by the influence of spiritual life in America. "It must never be forgotten," he wrote, "that religion gave birth to Anglo-American society. In the United States, religion is therefore mingled with all the habits of the nation and all the feelings of patriotism, whence it derives a peculiar force," writes Tocqueville. A significant example of this was the means used when facing a deadlock in framing America's constitution. The framers prayed. In the youngest nation of advanced countries of the world, from this crisis came the oldest democratic constitution for a republic in existence today.

And since that strong beginning, the importance of the influence of Jesus in American heritage appears in history books, except in recent ones rewritten to delete references to him. Early New England was permeated with the beliefs of Puritans, says Henry Bamford Parkes in the *The United States of America.* "Unlike the European peoples," Parkes writes in 1960, "the Americans were unified not by any community of ancestry and tradition but by common ideals and hopes for the future."

influence through individual believers

As stated earlier, progress in social spheres does not tell the real story of Jesus' influence. Institutions, even Christian ones, have no spiritual life apart from their leaders. Organizations, in fact, take upon themselves a life of their own after their founders die. Except for churches, most Christian-founded institutions can continue whether Christians or nonchristians carry them forward.

But Jesus did not come to establish an institution. He didn't die for an institution. Nor does Jesus any longer dwell in buildings. The New Testament says that he dwells in temples not made with hands, that believers themselves are temples of the Holy Spirit. Nor did Jesus come to start a "religion," as such. He pointed to Judaism as the true religion: "Salvation is of the Jews," [89] he told the woman at the well. He came not to abolish Judaism but to fulfill it, he said. In summary, Jesus' church is not a building, a religion, or an organization.

He came not to organize but to bring life. John says that Jesus told Nicodemus that unless he was born from above, he could not see the kingdom of God.[90] "He who has the Son has life; he who does not have the Son of God does not have life,"[91] the same apostle says. When the apostle Paul writes to different church groups, he speaks of the church, not as an organization, but as the living body of Christ.

Jesus' influence on society comes then through the heart change of individuals. Bill and a friend were two who found this new life in Jesus and passed it on to others. These two new Christians were so happy to be delivered from the grip of alcoholism that together they founded Alcoholics Anonymous. How many have watched their chains of addiction break and fall to the ground because of the influence of those two men!

In Bristol, England George Mueller was another individual who changed his world. In his care for hundreds of orphans, Mueller felt God wanted him not to solicit funds except in prayer. Because of his faith, thousands witnessed God's miraculous provision and believed. There were times when the orphans sat down for a meal with no food at hand; and then a delivery man or someone else brought an unexpected gift. Many were such crises. "I had a secret satisfaction," Mueller writes, "in the greatness of the difficulties. . . So far from being cast down on account of them, they delighted my soul. . . I did nothing but pray.* Prayer and faith. . . helped me over the difficulties."

*But Mueller was a man who worked diligently in the areas of his responsibilities.

Mueller's life reveals his confidence in God's call to the task; he knew he was only a "clay vessel." Like Paul he believed that "we have this treasure in earthen vessels, that the excellence of the power may be of God and not of us."[92]

And so through individuals Jesus changes even the fate of nations. He used Saint Augustine in North Africa, Martin Luther in Germany, John Calvin in Switzerland, John Knox in Scotland, and John Wesley in England. These clerics left not only an indelible mark upon their nations but also changed the way the world thinks and acts. And what about Jesus' influence through godly statesmen? Who can measure how far reaching that influence has been?

And Christian businessmen! How many have had an influence in that difficult arena where faith is sorely tested? And how many of them have used their resources to better the lives of others? "Businessmen are the one group that distinguish a free society from a totalitarian one," writes Ayn Rand.* The police state has farmers, doctors, engineers, soldiers, scientists, she observes, but no businessmen.

Also, worldwide Christian influence has helped stem the tide of totalitarianism. "It is no accident," says Walter Lippmann in *The Good Society*, "that the only open challenge to the totalitarian state has come from men of deep religious faith. For in their faith, they are vindicated as immortal souls, and from this enhancement of their dignity they find the reason why they must offer a perpetual challenge to the dominion of men over men."

For these tidechangers and pathmakers, Jesus leads the way. He laid down his life for his friends. "Greater love has no man," the Bible says. And Jesus continues to influence through those who follow this route, through those who lay down their lives to follow him.

influence in the world

How can persons of faith buck totalitarian governments? How could Mueller go out on a limb in trusting God to care for the orphans? How could Bill shed his shackles? How did Brother Lawrence walk in God's presence in the clatter of the kitchen and under the pressures of daily living? What gave the Shanxi Christians their courage? Yes, they all

*Ayn Rand article, "America's Persecuted Minority: Big Business," in *Capitalism*

received God's grace, but God prepared them another way. By his Word, he opened their eyes to see his kingdom in opposition to Satan's world system. They had the understanding that Jesus in his manifesto said was necessary to be fruitful in his kingdom: They understood spiritual warfare with the powers of darkness; they knew whose side they were on. And they were willing to die to themselves to seed a crop.

Though they did not encounter Marxist governments, they encountered the same antichristian spirit that prevails in every age. Jesus showed them that the world system is only temporary. In his manifesto, in fact, he says that it's doomed! sentenced! finished!—but that the kingdom of God is forever.

This understanding sets them free. No longer can the world attract or hold them. Hence, like Jesus, they can be *in* the world but not *of* the world. Theirs is a freedom that comes not from physical separation from the world but from the release of the heartstrings from attachment to that system. They disentangle themselves and plug into a different power source.

What freedom of power springs from their submission to God's authority! And how God weights their words! Jesus changed the destiny of these Christians separated to *his* power, authority, and teachings.* And by means of their influence, he made them destiny changers.

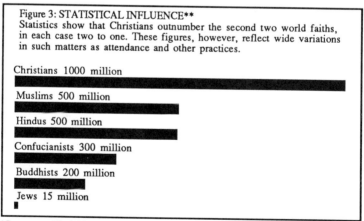

Figure 3: STATISTICAL INFLUENCE**
Statistics show that Christians outnumber the second two world faiths, in each case two to one. These figures, however, reflect wide variations in such matters as attendance and other practices.

Christians 1000 million

Muslims 500 million

Hindus 500 million

Confucianists 300 million

Buddhists 200 million

Jews 15 million

*See pages 85, 146   **facts from Jon Snow, *Atlas of Today*, Warwick ©1987

chapter 10. their polarity

their polarity

MARX OR JESUS

the basic conflict

Marx and Jesus open their windows to view a future world of peace, justice, and fulfillment. But one stands at the north pole and the other at the south. Down on the planet's playing field, their teams clash—in their foundations, their principles, their motives, their methods, their direction. "My bias against Christianity is so pronounced that I have a bias in favor of the apostate," Marx wrote Ferdinand Lassale in 1862. Although Marx sought the end result of what Jesus offers, he rejected Jesus' terms.

Marx also collides with Jesus' ethnic people. Another author could write a book, *Marx or Moses,* because Jews were Marx's special target, Saul K. Padover* says. "The charges Marx leveled against the people and the religion of at least twenty-five generations of his direct ancestors," Padover says, "have rarely been exceeded by any other serious writer in the field. He learned to despise and hate the people from whom he originated."

In Marx's materialist view, he established communism as atheistic and relegated the spiritual to the irrelevant, as something that will disappear on its own.

Marxist strategy: creating and controlling conflict

Warning: Class polarization in progress. World revolution, not war. —Wall Graffiti

To chart his map of the future, Marx looked to history, "science," nature, economics. Therefore, instead of meeting Jesus head on in the spiritual realm, Marx sidestepped. He set up a new center. By activating a political whirlpool, he set up a universe of his own making.

And with his personal bid for power, Marx set a pattern for his followers. He polarized issues and thus brought them to the fore. If in an organization he totally lost control, he caused it to disperse and in-

*Saul K. Padover, *Karl Marx on Religion.*

fluenced a new group. Or when necessary, he made alliances and bided his time until things went his way. In this way he guided the direction of the communist movement. And yet he held no official post of power except for a brief time in the International Working Men's Association. At the end of his life he had no organized following.

In similar ways, Marxist leaders seek to hasten historical progress. In a given country they create conditions to polarize people, bring them to revolution, and then grab from them the reins of power.

Marxist political activists, too, follow Marx's example; that is, to set up their own center, they politicize. To set the whirlpool in motion, they create discontent among society's disadvantaged and fringe persons by arousing them to blame the "haves" in government and business for making them "have-nots." Anger thus engendered in the "outs" brings forth destructive behavior, to which the "in" people, in turn, lash back. To that backlash, the underdogs react with hate and a greater sense of unjust treatment; now more than ever they feel justified in their opposition. And so the cycle continues.

By drawing their prey into this vortex, Marxists induce some of the bourgeois to join their side and provoke others to act in ways that will prove their villainy and incense the proletarians further. And so the pull of the whirlpool widens and strengthens. Sides polarize to further extremes and create a condition of instability. The communists, meanwhile, align themselves with all political parties on the left. And when instability peaks, they take control over both left and right.

In the strong pull of the whirlpool, Christians, too, find it difficult to sort out what is going on in order to know how to act intelligently and uprightly. In the process, if not drawn on the side of Marxism, many followers of Jesus fall into the snare of wrong attitudes and actions.

power, authority, teachings

*Power. . . authority. . . teachings!** These form the infrastructure Marx and Jesus both frame. Marx offers power over other men. He usurps authority by force and confiscation of property. He advocates principles that in practice lead to indoctrination by repetition, propa-

*See page 85, 142.

ganda, brainwashing. He justifies the means by the end. And, although Marx predicted the condition would be temporary, in the Soviet Union his teachings have led to permanent dictatorship, entrenched for over seventy years.

Jesus too offers power, but it is power to serve. Jesus' prescription differs from all others. Though the rest of the world counts greatness according to the measure of domination over others, Jesus says, "Yet it shall not be so among you; but whoever desires to become great among you, let him be your servant. And whoever desires to be first among you, let him be your slave—just as the Son of Man did not come to be served, but to serve."[93]

source and results

Though the ideal world held up by Marx and Jesus appears to be the same, the source and results of their "systems" differ in the following ways:

First their *personal lives* build on different authority. Marx rebels against God and marches under his own banner. He exalts man, who through labor will create a society of "new men" in harmony with the forces at work on this planet. To accomplish his goals, Marx promotes terrorism and makes no apology for the ruthlessness he claims for himself.* Jesus, in contrast, submits to his Father and to his instituted authority on earth. In his time here Jesus was the embodiment of humility.

Second, the *moral order* of the manifestos and principles of the two men derives authority from different sources. Marx bases his code on the absolute primacy of the communist movement; to this priority all other allegiances and relationships must yield. But Jesus founds his moral order on the absolutes of his Father in heaven. Marx, from his moral base, focuses on evolving class conflict; he sees the individual only as a part of the whole and as a product of each stage of history. But Jesus, from his moral base, is the expression of his Father's heart. He cares about the individual as the ultimate object of his concern and compassion. He says that for the individual and for society, all that is good or evil, comes from the human heart. With opposite moral bases,

*See page 23.

it's not surprising that college friend George Jung in 1841 said, "Marx calls Christianity one of the most immoral religions."

Third, the *community* that Marx and Jesus each offers bases itself on opposite principles of cause and effect. The community Jesus offers is a *result* of the association of transformed people with hearts filled with love, whereas the community Marx offers is the *cause,* the activating force for making "new men."

Fourth, facts about the *historical results* of the teachings of the two men are telling. Marx's basic premises and predictions fail, his regimes oppress, and his economies impoverish. Although Marxism is not the only active anti-God force in the world, it's one of the few that has governments and armies to back it up. Through its *teachings,* Marxism captures the hearts of men and through these men confiscates private property, whereby Marxist leadership gains the ownership and *authority* it needs to wield the *power* it wants. On the other hand, Jesus lives on through the contribution and example of individual Christians and in the change he brings to human society through them. America in its beginnings and early development is a prime example of the benefits of such influence on society.

in conclusion

In conclusion, the question of private or public ownership that Marx always raises is misleading. For the bottom line is not who owns property but who owns man. Does man, or an elite group of men in a party, own man? That is, do revolutionaries own those they "liberate"—even if only temporarily as a dictatorship—as Marx advocates? Or does God own man and offer him freedom, as Jesus says?

To whom does man owe his allegiance, Marx or Jesus? You can choose one, the other, or neither, but you can't choose both.

PART E
APPENDIX

scripture references
bibliography
index
acknowledgments
orderform

scripture references

chapter 1
1-KJV Matt. 6:22,23
2-John 10:10
3-Matt. 11:28, 29
4-John 10:30
5-John 8:58
6-NIV Matt. 20:15
7-Matt. 20:26
8-II Cor. 3:17
9-Gal. 5:1
10-James 1:25
11-Romans 8:21

chapter 6
12-Luke 2:51
13-Luke 16:12
14-John 7:26
15-John 7:46
16-John 18:6
17-Luke 10:19
18-Luke 20:4
19-Matt. 22:21
20-John 18:23
21-John 5:39,46
22-Luke 24:27
23-Romans 16:25,26
24-Luke 4:1
25-Psa. 22:28
26-John 5:19
27-Matt. 3:11
28-Matt. 3:15
29-Zech. 9:9
30-Mark 12:37
31-Luke 23:14
32-Matt. 27:18
33-Matt. 27:20
34-John 20:22
35-John 3:3

36-I Cor. 15:6
37-Acts 1:11
38-John 6:62
39-John 20:22
40-Matt. 28:18,19
    Acts 1:8

chapter 7
41-Mark 3:21
42-Gen. 18:18
43-I Cor. 10:32
44-Deut. 32:21
45-Rom. 11:11
46-Rom. 11:26
    Isa. 59:20,21
47-Mark 4:13
48-Gal. 5:22,23
49-Prov. 9:10
50-Prov. 20:27
51-Matt. 5:14,16
52-Mark 4:21
53-Acts 1:8
54-Matt. 18:17
55-Matt. 17:20
56-Matt. 16:18
57-Mark 4:32
58-Eph. 4:13
59-Judges 6:19
    I Sam. 1:24
60-I Cor. 5:7,8
61-Exod. 19:5,6
    Deut. 14:2
62-Psa. 135:4
63-Isa. 60:20,21
64-Matt. 15:24
65-Psa. 48:2

66-Psa. 105:43,44
67-Jer. 33:9
68-Heb. 12:2
69-Rom. 10:20
    Isa. 65:1
70-Matt. 18:11
71-John 1:14
72-Psa. 85:10,11
73-Luke 4:29

chapter 8
74-John 2:16
75-Isa. 56:7
    Mark 11:17
76-Jer. 7:11
    Matt. 21:13
77-Psa. 24:1
78-Rom. 13:2
79-Rom. 13:7
80-Acts 4:19,20
81-I Cor. 13:3
82-I Tim. 6:17
83-Matt. 19:21
84-Matt. 15:19
85-James 5:4
86-I Tim. 5:18
87-Col. 4:1

chapter 9
88-John 6:68
89-John 4:22
90-John 3:3
91-I John 5:12
92-II Cor. 4:7

chapter 10
93-Matt. 20:25-28

bibliography

Ailes, Roger. 1988. *You are the Message.* Dow Jones-Irwin. Homewood, Illinois

Alinsky, Saul D.1971. *Rules for Radicals: A pragmatic primer for realistic radicals.* New York

Archer, Fred. 1980. *"The Case of the Cagey Communist,"* a story from *Sir Lionel.* Costa Mesa, CA

Arendt, Hannah. 1951, 1958, 1966, 1968. *Totalitarianism: Part Three of the Origins of Totalitarianism.* New York

Bakker, J. I. (Hans). Number I. 1985. "Max Weber's Meta-Theory and Peace Research." National Perspectives, an Independent Journal of World Concerns

Barnet, Richard J. 1977. *The Giants: Russia and America.* New York

Bellah, R. N., R. Madsen, W. M. Sullivan, A. Swidler, S. M. Tipton. 1985. *Habits of the Heart: Individualism and commitment in American life.* New York

Benson, Peter L. and D. L. Williams. 1982. *Religion on Capitol Hill: Myths & realities.* San Francisco

Berger, Peter. 1986. *The Capitalist Revolution.* New York

Berle, Adolf A., Jr. 1954. *The 20th Century Capitalist Revolution.* New York

Berlin, Isaiah. 1963. *Karl Marx.* New York

Billington, James H. 1980. *Fire in the Minds of Men: Origins of the revolutionary faith.* New York

Bloom, Allan. 1987. *The Closing of the American Mind: how higher education has failed democracy and impoverished the souls of today's students.* New York

Blumenberg, Werner. 1972. *Portrait of Marx, an illustrated biography.* New York

Brennecke, John H.1971. *Significance: the struggle we share.* Beverly Hills

Brinton, Crane. 1938, 1952, 1965. *The Anatomy of Revolution.* New York

Bunzel, John, editor. 1988. *Political Passages.* New York

Chaney, David. 1979. *Fictions and Ceremonies. Representations of Popular Experience* (cultural studies). New York

Coleman, Richard J. 1972. *Issues of Theological Conflict: Evangelicals and Liberals.* Grand Rapids

Coolidge, Olivia. 1963. *Makers of the Red Revolution.* Boston

Cox, Harvey. 1984. *Religion in the Secular City: Toward a postmodern theology.* New York

DeKoster, Lester. 1956. *Communism & Christian Faith.* Grand Rapids

d'Encausse, Helene Carrere. 1982. *Confiscated Power: How Soviet Russia really works.* New York

Djilas, Milovan. 1957. *The New Class: An analysis of the communist system.* New York

Domhoff, G. William. *The Powers That Be: Processes of Ruling Class Domination in America.* New York

Douglas, J. D. 1974. *The New International Dictionary of the Christian Church.* Grand Rapids

Drucker, Peter F. 1976. *The Unseen Revolution: How pension fund socialism came to America.* New York

Eastman, Max. 1932. *Capital and Other Writings by Karl Marx.* New York

Ebenstein, William. 1962. *Two Ways of Life, the communist challenge to democracy.* New York

Ellul, Jacques. 1965. *Propaganda: The formation of men's attitudes.* New York

Fawcett, Edmund, M. 1982. *The American Condition.* New York

Filler, Louis. 1978. *Vanguards & Followers: Youth in the American tradition.* Chicago

Friedman, Milton. 1962. *Capitalism & Freedom: A leading economist's view of the proper role of competitive capitalism.* Chicago

Gilder, George. 1981. *Wealth & Poverty.* Toronto

Gilder, George. 1984. *The Spirit of Enterprise.* New York

Giroux, Henry A. 1988. *Schooling and the Struggle for Public Life.* Minneapolis

Goforth, Jonathan. 1942. Reprint 1962. *By My Spirit.* Minneapolis

Goldberg, George. 1984. *Reconsecrating America.* Grand Rapids

Gurley, John G.1988. *Challengers to Capitalism: Marx, Lenin, Stalin, and Mao.* A Portable Stanford Book. Reading, Massachusetts

Hawken, Paul. 1983. *The Next Economy*. New York
Heilbroner, Robert L. 1980. *Marxism: For and Against*. New York
Heilbroner, Robert L. 1953. 1986. *The Worldly Philosophies*. New York
Heller, Mikhail. 1988. *Cogs in the Wheel: The formation of Soviet Man*. New York
Hinchliff, Peter.1983. *Holiness and Politics*. Grand Rapids
Hirsch, Jr., E. D. 1987. *Cultural Literacy: what every American needs to know*. New York
Hook, Sidney. 1987. *Out of Step: An unquiet life in the 20th Century*. New York
Horn, Carl, ed. 1985. *Whose Values? The battle for morality in pluralistic America*. Ann Arbor,
    Michigan
Howard, John A. *Vital Speeches of the Day*, March 1, 1986: *"Disarming America's Will to Defend
    Itself."*
Howe, Irving, ed. 1983. *1984 Revisited: Totalitarianism in our century*. New York
Jackson, J. Hampden. Undated. *Marx, Proudhon, and European Socialism*. New York
Jaffe, Philip J. 1975. *The Rise and Fall of American Communism*. New York
Johnson, Paul. 1983. *Modern Times: The world from the twenties to the eighties*. New York
Kapp, Yvonne. 1976. *Eleanor Marx, Volume One* and *Volume Two*. New York
Kelso, James. 1969. *An Archeologist Looks at the Gospels*. Waco
Kietzman, Dale. 1986. *The Strategic Triangle: Time is running out!* World Literature Crusade
Kirk, Russell, ed. 1982. *The Portable Conservative Reader*.Penguin Books. New York
Kirk, Russell. 1951, 1964, 1978. *John Randolph of Roanoke: A Study in American politics*.
    Indianapolis
Knox, T. M., translator and commentator. 1952. *Hegel's Philosophy of Right*. London
Kraeling, Emil G., ed. 1959. *Historical Atlas of the Holy Land*. New York
Laski, Harold J. 1967. *Harold J. Laski on The Communist Manifesto*. New American Library. New
    York
Lekachman, Robert, B. VanLoon. 1981. *Capitalism for Beginners*. New York
Leone, Bruno. 1986. *Communism: Opposing viewpoints*. St. Paul, Minnesota
Lepp, Ignace. 1958. *From Karl Marx to Jesus Christ*. New York
Lippmann, Walter. 1943. *The Good Society*. New York
Lipson, Leslie. 1981. *The Great Issues of Politics*. New Jersey
Lyons, Eugene. 1937. *Assignment in Utopia*. New York
Madsen, Axel. 1980. *Private Power: Multinational Corporations for the Survival of Our Planet*. New
    York
Marx, Karl. 1965. *Selected Correspondence*. London
Mazour, Anatole G. and John M. Peoples. 1968. *Men and Nations, A World History*. New York
McLellan, David, editor. 1981. *Karl Marx: Interviews and Recollections*. Totowa, New Jersey
Mehring, Franz. 1962. *Karl Marx*. Ann Arbor
Meyer, Alfred G. 1970. *Marxism: The Unity of Theory and Practice. A Critical Essay*. Cambridge
Michaels, Leonard and Christopher Ricks. 1980. *The State of the Language*. Berkeley
Mill, John Stuart. 1975. *On Liberty*. New York
Miller, Lawrence M. 1984. *American Spirit: Visions of a new corporate culture*. New York
Mitton, C. Leslie. 1978. *Your Kingdom Come*. Grand Rapids
Morgan, G. Campbell. 1943. *The Parables and Metaphors of Our Lord*. Fleming H. Revell. New Jersey
Morison, James. 1981 Reprint. *Practical commentary on the Gospel According to St. Matthew*.
    Minneapolis
Naisbitt, John. 1984. *Megatrends: Ten new directions transforming our lives*. New York
Nash, George H. 1979. *The Conservative Intellectual Movement in America*. New York
Nave, Orville J. 1921. *Nave's Topical Bible*. Nashville
Oden, Thomas C. 1985. *Conscience and Dividends: Churches and the Multinationals*. Ethics and Public
    Policy Center. Washington, D.C.

Packard, Vance. 1959. *The Status Seekers: An exploration of class behavior in America.* New York
Padover, Saul K. 1974. *Karl Marx On Religion.* New York
The Phoenix.,Volume 6 Nos. 1 & 2 Summer/Fall 1977. Haydenville, Massachusetts
Parkes, Henry Bamford. 1960. *The United States of America: A History.* New York
Passell, Peter. 1986. *How to Read the Financial Pages.* New York
Payne, Robert. 1968. *Marx.* Simon and Schuster. New York
Powell, J. Enoch. "The Language of Politics"
Price, Walter K. 1972. *Jesus' Prophetic Sermon.* Moody. Chicago
Quinn, Daniel, Editor. 1972. *The Volume Library.* "The United Kingdom." Nashville
Raddatz, Fritz J. 1978. *Karl Marx: A Political Biography.* Boston
Rand, Ayn. 1946, 1962, 1964, 1965, 1966. *Capitalism: The unknown ideal.* New York
Rand, Ayn. 1982. *Philosophy: Who Needs It.* New York
Rand, Ayn. 1964. *The Virtue of Selfishness.* New York
Reeves, Richard. 1982. *American Journey: Traveling with Tocqueville in search of democracy in America.* New York
Revel, Jean-Francois. 1983. *How Democracies Perish.* New York
Rukeyser, Louis. 1983. *What's Ahead for the Economy.* New York
Russell, James. 1944. *Marx-Engels Dictionary.* Westport, Connecticut
Savage, Katherine. 1968. *The Story of Marxism and Communism.* New York.
Schnall, Maxine. 1981. *Limits: A search for new values.* New York
Shevchenko, Arkady N. 1985. *Breaking with Moscow.* New York
Shills, Edward. 1988. *Political Passages.* New York
Shultz, Richard H., Roy Godson. 1984. *Dezinformatsia: Active measures in Soviet strategy.* New York
Simon, William E. 1979. *A Time for Truth.* New York
Snow, Jon. *Atlas of Today.* Warwick Press. New York
Solinger, Dorothy. 1984. *Chinese Business Under Socialism: The politics of domestic commerce in contemporary China.* Berkeley
Solzhenitsyn, Aleksander I. 1975. *The Oak and the Calf: A memoir.* New York
Solzhenitsyn, Aleksander I. 1975, 1976. *Warning to the West.* Bodley Head Ltd. London
Sowell, Thomas. 1985. *Marxism: Philosophy and Economics.* New York
Sprigge, C. J. S. 1962. *Karl Marx.* New York
State Department. 1987. *Soviet Influence Activities: A report on active measures and propaganda, 1986-87.* Department of State Publication 9627. Washington, D. C.
Tarbell, Ida M. 1936, 1964, 1971. *The Nationalizing of business 1878-1898: A history of American life.* Chicago
Toffler, Alvin. 1980. *The Third Wave.* New York
Thomas, Cal. 1988. *The Death of Ethics in America.* Waco
Tyrell, R. Emmett, Jr. 1984. *The Liberal Crack-up.* New York
Universal Standard Encyclopedia. 1955. "Feudalism"; "Humanism"; "Manorialism"; "Middle Ages." New York
Walvoord, John F. 1974. *Matthew: Thy Kingdom Come.* Chicago
Ward, Barbara. 1959. *5 Ideas That Change the World.* New York
Weinberg, Sanford, ed. 1974, 1978, 1980. *Messages: A reader in human communication.* New York
White, Theodore H. 1982. *America in Search of Itself: the making of the president 1956-1980.* New York
Will, George F. 1983. *Statecraft as Soulcraft: What government does.* New York
Wilson, Colin. 1956, 1967. Introduction 1978. Foreword 1982. *The Outsider.* Los Angeles
World Book Encyclopedia.. 1974. Chicago.
Yarmolinsky, Avrahm. 1962. *Road to Revolution.* Toronto
Yoder, John Howard. 1984. *When War is Unjust: Being honest in just-war thinking.* Minneapolis

index

acknowledgments

I thank Warren Buffett. For "Chart 7: A Bourgeois View Of How the Market Works," quoted portions ©1988 by Warren E. Buffett are reproduced, with permission, from the 1987 Annual Report to Stockholders of Berkshire Hathaway, Inc.

I thank Rand McNally. The two map diagrams of the journeys of Jesus from *Rand McNally's Historical Atlas of the Holy Land* © 1959 are used with permission.

I thank the publishers of the New International Version and the publishers of the New King James Version for the right to quote portions of their translations of the Bible.

For other help, I thank family members and Paul Marciano, Cynthia Horkey, Steve Philo, Mary Reilly, Jeff Heitman, Suzann Kossian, Jean Maston, Harriet Acorne.

And for his steady hand, I thank the one about whom I write.

Small Helm Press interprets direction in contemporary life.

Forthcoming Book by Pearl Evans: **CHAMELEON TACTICS**
For information mark below.   *how liberation theology works*

1990: **THE PRACTICE OF THE PRESENCE OF GOD**
a classic by Brother Lawrence, a sixteenth century lay brother.
Practical but profound advice for modern life for one of any faith.

CHINA: THE LION AND THE DRAGON, by Pearl Evans
a personal interpretation of Chinese life, customs, history; a story by a
woman who lived/taught as only foreigner in college community.

FAITH'S CHECKBOOK by Charles H. Spurgeon.
New Topical Edition in modern English. Classic devotional:
365 scriptural promises and comments indexed to match your needs:
FOR GUIDANCE: when you ask why, when you worry about your children,
when friends betray you, when you feel hedged in, withdrawn, when you feel
abandoned, when you face business. . . AND MANY MORE

ORDER FORM   (707) 763-5757
                              Small Helm Press
                              622 Baker Street
                              Petaluma, California 94952
Please send me the following marked items:
_____ copies, MARX OR JESUS, hardcover   @$17.95
_____ copies, CHINA: The Lion and the Dragon, paperback @$14.95
_____ copies, FAITH'S CHECKBOOK, paperback   @$12.95
_____ Please send information about CHAMELEON TACTICS.
_____ I enclose COMMENTS on MARX OR JESUS.
In California only, with 6% tax, $15.85 CHINA; $13.73 FAITH; $19.33 MARX.
Shipping: hardcover $2.00 first copy, $1 each added book.
                  Paperback $1.50 first copy, $.50 each added book.
TOTAL ENCLOSED $ _____
I understand I may return any book for full refund if not satisfied.
NAME AND ADDRESS WITH ZIP: